CHRIST
AND RENAN

CHRIST AND RENAN

A COMMENTARY ON ERNEST RENAN'S "THE LIFE OF JESUS"

BY
M. J. LAGRANGE, O.P.

TRANSLATED BY
MAISIE WARD

WIPF & STOCK · Eugene, Oregon

Wipf and Stock Publishers
199 W 8th Ave, Suite 3
Eugene, OR 97401

Christ and Renan
A Commentary on Ernest Renan's "The Life of Jesus"
By Lagrange, M. J.
ISBN 13: 978-1-60608-392-5
Publication date 12/30/2008
Previously published by Sheed & Ward, 1928

Nihil obstat: Georgius D. Smith, S.T.D.
Censor Deputatus
Imprimatur: Edm : Can : Surmont.
Vic. Gen.
Westmonasterii, die 8° Octobris, 1928.

CONTENTS

TRANSLATOR'S NOTE

My thanks are due to Messrs. J. M. Dent & Sons, publishers of the *Everyman Library*, for permission to use their Translations for the quotations from Renan's *Life of Jesus*. Père Lagrange quoted from the 13th or definitive French edition which is fuller than the one used for the *Everyman* edition. When obliged to have recourse to this I have indicated it by putting "French edition." All other page numbers refer to the *Everyman* edition.

One or two dates have been omitted, and one or two sentences in the text, as being of interest only to French readers.

In the translation of Renan's book, small letters are invariably used for pronouns referring to Our Lord. I have adhered to this also when paraphrasing Renan's remarks, for, as Père Lagrange points out, the Jesus of Renan is not "The Jesus Christ of Catholics."

CHRIST AND RENAN

RENAN, turned jester at the end of his life, was pleased to say " A really complete work should need no refutation. The error contained in each thought should be so well indicated that the reader may take in at a glance the two opposite aspects which make up every truth."[1]

When he wrote the *Life of Jesus*, Ernest Renan was undoubtedly imbued with that accommodating philosophy which knows how to combine contradictions. He was, however, very far from that detachment from his own opinions, which he later affected. Rather he proposed to restore to his own generation the pure religion of Jesus, Whose picture he painted in hours of enthusiasm, believing that he had found Him still discoursing on the hills of Galilee, or from His boat upon the lake. Renan's art stripped exegesis of the heavy garments with which the climate of Germany had smothered it, and robed it in a white tunic from the east. His success was immense, and the sensation still continues.

It is not customary among critics to discuss Renan's views. Specialists do not take him very seriously. Nevertheless the *Life of Jesus* has reached

[1] *Le prêtre de Nemi*, p. vii.

its fifty-second edition—and to this must be added twenty editions of the *Vie Populaire.* Renan's other works have not had such vogue.

If certain more studious men of learning have gone farther than he in their contempt for tradition, they have not, merely by so doing, won public favour. There must be in this morally ugly work some quality that makes people love it. At a moment when Germany seemed to have exhausted the cycle of every possible combination to explain the fact of Jesus, people wanted to know the solution offered by a mind very detached, very penetrating, disciple of the German critics (a fact Renan did not hide), but still very French. He was French in a certain grasp of concrete reality, and in a sense of proportion which kept him safe from the excesses which marred the theories of his masters beyond the Rhine. It is not enough to denounce Renan to French public opinion as a Bosch. If he had been one altogether, Paris would not have enjoyed him so much. At the time when the *Life of Jesus* appeared Catholics were deeply stirred by its denial of Christ's divinity, a denial so sweeping that it was put forward as an ascertained fact, and no trouble was taken to discuss it. Bishops, priests, even laymen took up the defence of the faith. So, long after, we still have the same feeling of disgust, but we do not want to do over again what was then done well. Renan did not choose to "condescend" to that controversy, and the time to draw him into it is over. But time has done its work, and has ranged the *Life of Jesus* among the numerous attempts to solve an enigma which for those outside the faith always remains insoluble, and is in very truth " a sign of contradiction." Yet it is not without interest for us to see why this effort failed like the rest. It had so many chances of success:—the accumulation of a century of preparatory work, the effect of surprise in a conjuring exhibition, the resources of science, and the charms of art. And why should we not acknowledge also a sound element in this historical examination, which can still be used in apologetics, provided we exclude what is merely arbitrary?

This is the task attempted in the following pages. They do not contain a complete critical examination, as the only means of carrying this out would be to annotate a text which we have no right to reproduce. We will merely first point out the antecedent bent of the author's mind, which imposed the method pursued and even the main conclusion, and then indicate the broad lines of literary criticism and of the historical method, with their application both to the Mission and the Person of Jesus and to His miracles.

I

Antecedent Leanings, Negative Prejudice, and Positive Aspiration

From the very first, and in explaining his method, Renan is determined to distinguish himself from the German schools. And, in fact, the *Life of Jesus* was only discussed in Germany during the nineteenth century by theologians. The eighteenth century had seen the Orientalist, Reimarus, rejected by the theologians as a deist. Certainly these theologians did not resemble ours. They were emancipated enough to write "the gospel according to Hegel."

But they did remain more or less attached to Protestant Evangelicalism, and, anxious not to break with the gospels, they were content to eliminate whatever seemed to them intolerable to the modern world. Bruno Bauer had broken a lance with all Christian tradition, but he was still dogmatic, with the dogmatism of hate. Renan would not hear of dogma of whatever kind.

"The theologian is an interested party because of his dogma. Reduce this dogma as far as you will, it still remains for the artist and the critic a weight insupportable. . . . Let us announce boldly: critical studies relating to the origins of Christianity will only say their last word when they are cultivated in a purely laic and secular spirit, after the methods of the Hellenists, the students of Arabic and Sanscrit, who, strangers to all theology, think neither of edifying nor of scandalising, neither of defending dogmas nor of overthrowing them."[1]

We sincerely wish that non-Christians *would* approach the origins of Christianity in this spirit, provided only that they are also prepared to accept the supernatural if the evidence is strong enough. But Renan was far removed from this impartiality: "To write the history of a religion it is necessary, firstly, to have believed it (otherwise we should not be able to understand how it has charmed and satisfied the human conscience[2]); in the second place to believe it no longer in an absolute manner, for absolute faith is incompatible with sincere history."[3]

Notice first the degree of discernment he awards himself as a former seminarist; yet observe also that even complete antecedent negation gives no guarantee of impartiality. Often as Renan has changed his opinions, there is one point on which

[1] p. x, French edition.

[2] p. 31. The scruple is touching. But Mgr. Dupanloup recognised another note when he observed "It was again in reference to the unfortunate Lamennais that M. Renan wrote that those who come forth from the sanctuary and make war on *the dogma that they have served* have, in the blows that they strike, *a sure hand that the layman can never attain, a special note of coolness and assurance. . . . the audacity of an intimate. Avertissement à la Jeunesse*, etc., p. 110, quoting *Essais*, p. 141, 2.

[3] p. 31.

he has never changed. He, too, has a *Credo* to which he has held unswervingly—the denial of the supernatural. And by the supernatural he does not only mean miracles, prophecies, and sacraments, but even the existence of a God distinct from the world. He rejected atheism as being bad taste, deism as too narrow a conception, and if he believed that a superior mind should not rank itself with the pantheists it was because he wished to retain the use of the word "God" as a "Category of the Ideal."

Moreover, these discussions on deism and pantheism serve only "little minds." "Were the men who have best comprehended God—Sakya-Mouni, Plato, St. Paul, St. Francis d'Assisi, and St. Augustine (at some periods of his fluctuating life)—deists or pantheists? Such a question has no meaning."[1] But if he thought it worthy of himself to float above these questions in which the "little minds" of Spinosa and Hegel exhausted themselves (for these men did count for him although he would have rejected Descartes and Bossuet, Pascal and St. Thomas Aquinas) Renan did set forth in a purely Oriental form his conviction of how God came to be. "Humanity makes divinity as the spider spins its web."[2]

When then, rejecting "individual supernatural facts," he claims to maintain "the supernatural in

[1] p. 69.

[2] *Job* XL. Or less poetically "The universal work of all living things being to make a perfect God . . . reason . . . will one day undertake the supervision of this great work, and after organising humanity, will organise God." (*L'Avenir de Science*, p. 37).

general," he is simply yielding to the prepossession for keeping Catholic words but using them with a purely Hegelian meaning. He remarked of Feuerbach that he was not an atheist, but rather a religious man, or that if he were an atheist it was after the German fashion, "devoutly and with unction."[1]

Later on he laughed at himself, and at this unction, but at first he did not laugh; he believed he had a mission, and he had no tenderness for the Catholicism he had abandoned. He believed the Church irrevocably lost. "The temples of Jesus, truly present, will crumble; the tabernacles believed to contain his flesh and blood will be shattered. Already the roof is open to the daylight, and the rain of heaven wets the face of the kneeling believer."[2]

Was Renan then in the frame of mind of a historian who thinks "neither of defending dogmas nor of upsetting them"? On the contrary, all his philosophical remarks witness to a lofty assurance, an absolute conviction. God, being at the term of human activity, how could He have intervened in the course of history? His mind was so thoroughly secularised that it necessarily assumed the denial of Christian dogma. He retained only the equivocal use of the *word* "God"—an old word, a little heavy, perhaps, but which has on its side "a long prescriptive right; to suppress it would be to throw humanity out of its track, and to separate oneself in

[1] *Liberté de Penser*, vol. VI, p. 347.
[2] *Liberté de Penser*, Vol. III, p. 470.

speech from the simple beings who adore so well after their fashion."[1]

Language then does not express thought—at any rate when God is mentioned. It was necessary to remind the reader of these sayings, before reading this *Life of Jesus*, where sincerity is paraded so prominently, the conscience of the man of to-day distinguished from that of the Oriental, or even, we are forced to say, the sincerity of Jesus distinguished from that of His critical historian. Renan's reproach to Lamennais must also be weighed—that he "did not understand the irony of a certain sort of respect."[2]

Sceptics, advanced free thinkers, but men who do stop short somewhere, have pointed this out exactly like Catholic apologists. "It may be a little overdoing it," writes M. Séailles in the same ironic and measured style, "to attribute motives to a God who does not exist. Renan misuses mythology; he creates beings out of words."[3] Mgr. Dupanloup had said more simply, "He speaks like you, but does not think like you."[4]

On this point every one agrees—Renan first excluded God from history and then spoke of Him as if He existed. What did the word religion mean for him?

About this, too, he was definite enough. God being "The Category of the Ideal," religion was that part of the ideal to which souls offer sacrifice. For him this was science, for others whatever they

[1] *Etudes*, p. 419.

[2] *Essais*, p. 187.

[3] *Ernest Renan*, p. 282, note 2.

[4] *Avertissement*, p. 15.

loved best. Towards the end of his life he described this religion in a brutal formula, in words unworthy of his grey hairs. "The means of salvation are not the same for all. For one it is virtue; for another passion for truth; for another love of art; for others curiosity, ambition, travel, luxury, women, wealth; in a lower stage morphine and alcohol; the most dangerous mistake in social morality is the systematic suppression of pleasure."[1]

Must we say that this was simply lifting his mask and revealing what had always been at the bottom of his mind? Was his determination to speak as others spoke without thinking as they thought merely hypocrisy? Surely not, for a mere hypocrite would have gone straight forward for the priesthood without a shudder, like Paul de Gondi, the future Cardinal de Retz. Whence then the posture into which he forced himself, of calling himself religious, Christian even, and true disciple of Jesus?

Was it that at the bottom of his soul the religious sentiment persisted, the remains of tenderness towards the God who had been the joy of his youth? Yet, this God did not exist!

On leaving the seminary Renan became what he always remained, a convinced devotee of science. Science was to him his particular Category of the Ideal. If he tinged it with religiosity was it merely that he might not turn towards gross scepticism? It may well be. It always disgusted this acute and subtle nature to ally himself with the group of free-

[1] *Feuilles détachées*, p. 382.

thinkers who went the further length of emptying their glasses in honour of Béranger's god of good fellows. But he might have stood alone.

Nor was his religious affectation a form of diplomatic prudence, necessary at a time when those in power listened to the voice of the bishops,—for he faced the storm and bore with dignity the imperial disfavour.

He must then have been in mind undecided enough to rest satisfied with vague ideas, but in character firm enough never to disclaim what had been his thought. He certainly knew how much he changed, but he stuck fast to a certain basis, and, having reduced his ideal to nothing but a vague love of truth, he could claim to have always been faithful to it. Why did he always keep the words—God, religion, and even in that last epicurean baseness the expression "to win salvation," except to avoid having disowned his original position?

And for the same reason he clung to his official admiration for Jesus. The lower he got on the slope which brought the former philosopher of the ideal down to the encourager of a debauchery which Epicurus would have rejected, the deeper and more horrifying became the gulf between his wanton toasts and his former gravity. When he began, and even when he was writing the *Life of Jesus* Renan still believed in the pure religion of the Ideal, and he attributed its origin to Jesus Christ.

It was assuredly a strange state of mind, an enigma for Frenchmen, and only to be explained by his attachment to German theology from the moment he left the seminary. He was careful to let us know that his faith was destroyed by historical criticism, not by philosophy. In company with more than one Catholic writer, M. Séailles refuses to believe this.

"The truth is," he writes, "that in 1843, at the end of his stay at Issy, when he knew neither Hebrew nor German, and had read neither Gesenius nor Ewald, he found in his reason alone a dangerous enemy to his faith."[1] In fact, one might readily say with M. Cognat, that "Hebrew is even more innocent than woman of his intellectual emancipation"[2]. But Renan was able to read in French the *Life of Jesus*, by Strauss, for Littré had just translated it.

Without disparagement of his marvellous talent, it may be said that Renan had not a philosophical mind. His impertinent claim to have mastered problems over which great geniuses exhaust themselves, is in fact an admission of incompetence. Philosophical objections affected him. But he viewed them in a fashion which tried to reconcile them with religion, giving up, indeed, the definite faith of Christians, but without abjuring Jesus Christ. The morality of Kant re-assures him, but Kant does not save Christ for him, and he still clings to keeping Christ. "I have been studying Germany, and I felt as though entering into a temple. Everything I found there was pure, exalted, moral,

[1] *Ernest Renan*, p. 17.

[2] Quoted by M. Séailles, op. cit. p. 17.

beautiful and touching. Oh my soul, we have found a treasure, the continuation of Jesus Christ. Their goodness overwhelms me: how sweet and strong they are! I think Christ will come to us from there. This vision of a new spirit seems to me an event similar to the birth of Christianity. . . . France seems to me more and more a country utterly empty of all share in the great work of the renewal of life in the human race. . . . Jesus Christ is nowhere to be found there."[1] This new life was, without doubt, that Hegelian conception to which Strauss had dedicated Christ as a type of God's union with man.

Renan, leaving the seminary definitely because he had lost his faith, was about to enter the world with a new faith, which allowed him still to speak of God and of religion, and to call himself a Christian. It is not mere pleasantry when he states "that the world will be eternally religious and that christianity, in a broad sense, is the last word in religion."[2]

By this remains of religious sentiment (of a very modern kind), almost as much as by his sweeping denial of the supernatural, he failed in the *rôle* he claimed of an impartial historian. Liberal Protestantism, Renan said, was incapable of writing the *Life of Jesus* because it still contained too much dogma. But he did not realise that he, too, had a dogma, the dogma of pure religion, without altars, without priests, without observances—

[1] *Souvenirs*, p. 385.

[2] *Questions Contemporaines*, p. 337.

not that religion preached by the deists, but that which might have been conceived by a Hegelian absorbed in developing and "organising God."

This is indeed a thesis—the thesis of the *Life of Jesus*. "'Christianity' has thus become almost a synonym of 'religion.' All that is done outside of this great and good Christian tradition is barren. Jesus gave religion to humanity as Socrates gave it philosophy. . . . Jesus founded the absolute religion, excluding nothing, and determining nothing unless it be the spirit [*sentiment*]."[1] "Whatever revolution takes place will not prevent us attaching ourselves in religion to the grand intellectual and moral line at the head of which shines the name of Jesus. In this sense we are Christians."[2] He repeats this constantly, without troubling to change his formulæ greatly. "A pure worship, a religion without priests and external observances, resting entirely on the feelings of the heart, on the imitation of God, on the direct relation of the conscience with the heavenly Father, was the result of these principles."[3] "It has been by the power of a religion free from all external forms that Christianity has attracted elevated minds."[4] "He founded the pure worship of all ages, of all lands, that which all elevated souls will practise until the end of time."[5] "It was a pure religion, without forms, or temple, or priest; it was the world's moral judgment delegated to the conscience of the just and the arm of the people."[6]

[1] *Life of Jesus*, pp. 236–7. [2] *Life of Jesus*, p. 237. [3] p. 73. [4] p. 86. [5] p. 140. [6] p. 162.

Clearly it is almost a monomania, and surely a sort of dogma—the positive complement of his denial of the supernatural. It would be strange if this dogma, which has to be proved, as it has not been revealed, had not affected the impartiality of the historian. As a matter of fact, Renan does not insist greatly on the positive side of his views. His formula, as we have seen, is supremely negative—the exclusion of external worship and of priesthood. He was inspired by the Hegelian idea of becoming—an idea as old as Heraclitus. The possibility of bringing contradictions into harmony suited his humour. But he had not resolutely accepted the identity of contradictions in the Idea which existed before the facts. Nor had he assented to the practical results according to Hegel, who had given a massive solidity to the Idea in the shape of the Prussian state. Renan's Idea was intangible, incorporeal, up in the air to such an extent that religion itself had to be robbed of all external support. All this means that his pure religion was also individualistic, and it was as such that it was understood and enjoyed in France. Who among us Frenchmen is seriously concerned in co-operating in the formation and organisation of the divine? But we still remembered the natural religion of Voltaire, and Renan lent a charm to this dry and unpoetic creed. In his own way he harmonised Voltaire and Rousseau. His rigid exclusion of the supernatural, of mystery, and of miracle satisfied the all too genuine French inclination for clear-cut ideas even if they lack height and depth; his moral sentiment satisfied the heart. Unhappily Renan from this time onwards was far below Rousseau in his sincere respect for the "holiness" of the Gospel. "Holiness" is not the atmosphere of the *Life of Jesus*. Such as he was, the ideal of the book was *his* ideal, and was that which he offered to the age he lived in. He loudly proclaimed the hope (and he was still sincere) of saving thereby whatever in religion is absolute and eternal—or rather whatever is of relative use now and in future. . . . anyhow for the simple. This design is somewhat analogous to that of liberal Protestantism: it is only one degree lower in the amount of Christianity it contains. But it is only a question of degree. Resolved to reject the supernatural, and to look upon Jesus as the founder of "his" religion, he risked misunderstanding or even wilfully distorting the past. Renan was not the impartial historian that he claimed to be. Not to omit a shading off, which in his case would be serious, we must add to this the fact that his unbending principle was always varied by flights of fancy. But there remained always that aversion from the supernatural which was for this Breton the granite foundation of all thought. But he managed to escape from that systematic mentality that exposes many a German building, erected strictly according to rule, to a complete crash. History abhors contradictory assertions as much as philosophy, but the historian who knows how to measure his strength is modest in his assertions, and very often refuses to assert anything. As for Renan, he looked on contradictions as alternative ways of reaching truth. He carried this too far, but we shall have to note that his tact as a historian often saved him from sacrificing views which a more rigid mind must have excluded to safeguard the unity of his work.

II

Literary Criticism of the Gospels. Other Sources

This is not Renan's most original chapter. Or rather we may say that in it he shows himself more personal in his conclusions than in the steps that lead up to them. Despite appearances, a man may give proof of originality, or if you prefer, of acuteness, in analysing the relations of the gospels to each other so as to deduce the character of their composition. This is literary criticism, and it may serve as a basis to historical criticism. At the time at which Renan wrote this sort of work had long been on the stocks in Germany, and he did not think it wise to begin it over again, especially in relation to the first three, or synoptic gospels. He was obliged to explain in more detail, that he might defend it, the special position he took up in regard to the fourth gospel.[1]

Strauss had got on to a wrong tack in his theory about the compilation of the gospels, and this Renan realised—and realised more clearly as the "Mark hypothesis" continued to gain ground in Germany.

[1] We are only speaking here of the gospels as the basis of the *Life of Jesus*, not of Renan's book *Les Evangiles et la seconde génération chrétienne*.

In the preface to the thirteenth edition he wrote: "More and more Mark seems to me the primitive type of the synoptic narratives, and the text with most authority."[1]

But he did not trouble to go into the analysis of Weisse in any detail, and it is undoubtedly to the dominant current of liberal criticism that he adhered, at the time of the reaction against Strauss and Bruno Bauer.

What was his view of the origin of the first three biographies of the Saviour, if that title may be given to the synoptics? He does not conceal his prejudices. "That the gospels are in part legendary is evident, since they are full of miracles, and of the supernatural."[2] But even this tribute to the prejudice of rationalism is not enough, he must also give in to the craze for popular creation: "The most beautiful thing in the world has thus proceeded from an obscure and purely popular elaboration."[3] This means, no doubt, that the gospels are, as Strauss saw them, the work of the community? No, Renan's mind was too acute to accept without caution this bit of higher critical imagination.

The result is that his assertion of a completely popular elaboration remains absolutely in the air, for it is no proof to assert that changes were afterwards introduced into the existing text of the gospels. "At that time," says Renan, "the spirit was everything; the letter was nothing."[4] Why then explain

[1] p. xiii, French edition.
[2] p. 7.
[3] p. 10.
[4] p. 10.

the popular elaboration of the gospels from the fact that "The poor man who has but one book wishes that it may contain all that is dear to his heart. These little books were lent; each one transcribed in the margin of his copy the words and the parables he found elsewhere, which touched him."[1]

Clinging to the spirit then did not prevent them from clinging to the letter? In fact, the Christian people showed from the beginning an immense desire to know what Jesus had said and done, and it was to satisfy this desire that the gospels were written. Only, those who were questioned were those who had seen, who preached, who taught, and who were the actual heads of the community. It was also their *rôle* to write.

Renan, in fact, finds no difficulty in recognising in the second gospel Peter's memoirs.

The passage does honour to his critical sense, and is still of value against much more daring negations.

"In Mark the facts are related with the clearness for which we seek in vain among the other evangelists. He likes to report certain words of Jesus in Syro-Chaldean. He is full of minute observations,[2] coming doubtless from an eye-witness. There is nothing to prevent our agreeing with Papias in regarding this witness, who evidently had followed Jesus, who had loved him, and observed him very closely, and who had

[1] Same page!

[2] It is true that elsewhere (p. 8) Mark "is brief even to dryness."

preserved a lively image of him, as the Apostle Peter himself."[1]

All the same Renan does not consider that our second gospel is the primitive gospel of Mark. For this he gives a double-edged reason, which can scarcely prove at one and the same time, that both the first and the second gospels have been profoundly altered. Following the German critics, he regards the first gospel as a biography added to the sayings, or *Logia*, collected by the Apostle Matthew—less a " man of the people " than the rest of the apostolic group. Without reopening the discussion on this question of the *Logia*, we may admit that the first gospel is not absolutely in its primitive state, since it has been translated from the Aramaic. Renan reasoned thus, "In the present state of the texts, the ' Gospel according to Matthew ' and the ' Gospel according to Mark ' present parallel parts, so long and so perfectly identical that it must be supposed, either that the final compiler of the first had the second under his eyes, or *vice versa*, or that both copied from the same prototype."[2]

This leaves us a choice, and if I choose the first hypothesis, clearly I can deduce nothing from the two others which no longer apply. Renan then has no right to conclude " that which appears the most likely is that we have not the entirely original compilations of either Matthew, or Mark, but that our first two gospels are versions in which the attempt is made to fill up the gaps of the one text by the

[1] pp. 20, 21. [2] p. 9.

other. . . . He who had in his copy only discourses wished to have narratives, and *vice versa*."[1] *Vice versa*? But if the primitive Mark—the Mark of Papias—had the facts and the discourses (λεχθέντα ἢ πραχθέντα) what had he to borrow from the Aramaic or the Greek Matthew? And supposing that Mark consulted a collection of discourses, a hypothesis very difficult to verify, and which Renan never investigated, could he not have arrived in one step at the result that we know?

The literary unity of Mark is no less certain than that of the fourth gospel. Moreover, we know that up-to-date criticism is no longer so certain that the first gospel contained only discourses. But as Renan did nothing to establish the secondary character of the Greek Matthew, there is no point in continuing the discussion.

As a man of letters he clung especially to the third evangelist, in whom he recognised a more personal attraction, one would almost say a brother in the art of writing! He certainly could, by no possibility be a fictitious, anonymous being, a popular creation. His personality is even so marked that Renan unhesitatingly attributes to him the Acts of the Apostles also. He wrote not long after the siege of Jerusalem, and is later than the first two evangelists. Here we are far from the dates postulated by the criticism of Strauss, and this time Renan may be counted among the defenders of traditions.

[1] p. 9.

He was then arriving at a general view of the synoptics. The first two he considers have gone successively through two different stages: that of the original documents, first editions which exist no longer, then the stage of a simple mixture, in which the original documents are put together with no attempt at arrangement, and in which can be seen no glimpse of the personal outlook of the authors (the existing gospels of Matthew and of Mark). Luke inaugurates a new method—the stage of combination of deliberate and thoughtful editing in which we perceive an effort to conciliate the different versions. The third stage includes—he does really say it—the gospel of Luke, the gospels of Marcion, Tatian, etc.[1]

A few reflections must be made about all this.

We will not cavil over these editions which exist no longer, for, if they have only been amalgamated do they not still exist in a state of fusion?[2] Renan, however, puts at the beginning what belongs to the end—Tatian's amalgamation. And can it really be said that, in contrast to Luke, the first two evangelists have no personal outlook? Did not the first aim at proving that the prophecies were fulfilled in Jesus, the second at proving by his miracles that He was the Son of God. This remark is all the more disinterested on our part, because the simple mixture without personal outlook would seem to give promise of greater candour. But still one may have an aim and yet be honest in pur-

[1] p. lxxxvii, French edition.

[2] And this, too, is what we read in the Introduction.

suing it. Renan characterises Luke badly enough, even as a writer. He sees in the third gospel " the work of a man who selects, prunes, and combines."[1]

Let it be agreed that he chooses and prunes, and then no one has the right to say that the primitive Mark did not contain passages which are not in Luke. But does he combine? Has he made an effort to conciliate the different versions? And are those the versions we know? But he certainly does not depend on Matthew. Are they then versions we do not know? In that case what do we know about them? And this comparison of the Luke who " conciliates," with Marcion? Did Marcion combine so as to be put between Luke and Tatian? On the contrary, he pruned, and, as far as we know, the only text he pruned was that of Luke. Is it not strange to give Tatian the third place in this series? He certainly combined: that is indisputable! But the Church did not accept his combination. And with what view did he make it? The critics would not be sorry if they could find out.

The conciliating combinations of Luke may well only be a reminiscence of Bauer. Renan has another reproach to make against Luke. Some sentences are " distorted and exaggerated," and in other places " he subdues some details in order to make the different narratives agree." As an example of the first, Luke made Jesus say, " He who hates not his father and mother," etc. (Luke xiv, 26), a saying too hard for the " Charmer " of

[1] p. 7.

Galilee, but in which the critics recognise the primitive note softened by Matthew (x, 37)—although they *might* explain it by the abrupt antitheses always found in Semitic languages. In the second case of pretended concordance, Luke (iv, 16) departs from Mark without getting any nearer to Matthew. The chief grievance against Luke, his determination to go to meet the sinner, is no better established. It is on this account that he is supposed to have transformed the scene of the anointing of the feet of Jesus into a scene of pardon. "Finally, he has, in the narrative of the last hours of Jesus, some circumstances full of tender feeling, and certain words of Jesus of delightful beauty, which are not found in more authentic accounts, and in which we detect the presence of legend."[1] What is here very characteristic of Renan, is this sigh of the critic obliged to sacrifice some words of "delightful beauty."

But what compels him to do so? These violent excisions are the act of an advanced critic, determined to exclude all that appears to be later than his concept of the first two gospels, as suspect of being adventitious and imaginary. But Renan is not in that position. With rare insight he has pointed out many passages where the tradition followed by Luke is conciliated, without apparent effort, without any indication of a policy, with the exposition of the fourth gospel.[2] His last words on Luke, therefore, leave us perplexed; he is, we are told, a "harmoniser,"

[1] p. 22. [2] p. 213, note 1, French edition.

"a corrector after the manner of Marcion and Tatian."

This sentence, which puts two extreme opposites into one group, has really no sense. Nevertheless, "he is a biographer of the first century, a divine artist, who, independently of the information which he has drawn from more ancient sources, shows us the character of the founder with a happiness of treatment, with a uniform inspiration, and a distinctness which the other two synoptics do not possess."[1]

Renan followed tradition much more in his appreciation of the fourth gospel, showing himself less dependent on the German critics, and less slave to a system than they. Feeling himself in disagreement with an opinion which greatly affected him, he made a point of giving his reasons. We must not expect his position to be clear-cut, and if he felt obliged to yield little by little to the movement which was carrying all before it in Germany, the concession was in appearance only. It seemed too unpopular to maintain, even with many attenuations, the authenticity of the fourth gospel. According to the first edition of the *Life of Jesus* this gospel is in the main by the apostle John, although it may have been re-edited and re-touched by his disciples. From the thirteenth edition onwards it is no longer the work of John the son of Zebedee. It was attributed to him by one of his disciples, towards the year 100. Looking at the question from the point of view of the historian, we may say that the essen-

[1] p. 22.

tial thing was to uphold the traditional character of the discourses. This excludes, first of all, the opinion inaugurated by Strauss, for a short while abandoned by him, and then taken up again, dominating in independent criticism, which makes of the fourth gospel a work of pure theology, an allegory under a veil of history, written towards the middle of the second century. As to the historicity of the facts Renan remained in agreement with Catholic opinion, but he denied that the discourses of the fourth gospel represented the thought of Jesus.

All the same, everything must not be rejected in the discourses, and not all the facts are true history. This is one of the points on which Renan kept most freedom for himself, shading off his contradictions with the utmost care. Had he good reasons for making these changes? If the historical tradition goes back to John he is still in a certain sense the author of the gospel, more especially as the first edition did not attribute to him the editing properly so-called. And even after making his corrections, Renan did not admit the existence of the presbyter John as distinct from the apostle.[1] He would not adopt this as the explanation of why tradition was so strong on the name of John. He tried to get over it in two ways: by contesting in a quite arbitrary

[1] P. lxxii, French edition. The presbyter John must have been invented so as to attribute the Apocalypse to another than John the Apostle. In the text of Papias the words ἢ τὶ Ἰωάννης must on this theory have been interpolated. This is a direct blow to the theory revived by M. Harnack; but there is absolutely nothing to lend colour to the hypothesis of an interpolation.

manner the authenticity of the epistle of St. Polycarp and the passages of the epistles of St. Ignatius, where allusions are found to the fourth gospel;[1] secondly, by imagining that John the son of Zebedee, having fallen into a state of feebleness, in which he was, in a measure, at the mercy of his entourage, "a secretary might profit from that state to make him whom everybody called 'the old man' (ὁ πρεσβυτερος) speak in his characteristic fashion."[2]

His kindly thought was to suppose a disrespectful trick played on an old man as the origin of the fourth gospel! And there was nothing to be scandalised about. "This is not the only instance of an heretical book forcing the gates of the orthodox church and becoming the rule of faith."[3]

This assertion did not apparently require the establishing or even the indication of any proof. A well-chosen reason points to the date as being before the year 100. "After that date it is no longer conceivable that the author should so have freed himself from the framework of the 'Apostolic Memoirs.'"[4] This argument, however, proves too much: even at that date a book would not have been received placing the history of Jesus in so different a frame from that of the synoptics, had it not been composed by an eye-witness, or at any rate confirmed by a very high authority. Who could that authority be but John, the last survivor among the apostles? And if it had not been received

[1] p. 11. [2] p. 16. [3] p. 17. [4] p. 17.

at that date, still less would it be received later. The quotation from Papias is really only a clipping from Eusebius. Because it does not mention the fourth gospel Renan has no right to conclude absolutely that Papias had no knowledge of it.[1]

It is clear from the text that the reproach that Mark did not follow the exact order of events was not made by a defender of St. Matthew's chronology, nor could it come from a defender of Luke's, which is the same as Mark's. It must then come from a comparison of the chronology of the respective texts of Mark and John. That of Mark is, on the whole, abandoned, since excuses are made for it. It is most probably in favour of the chronology of the fourth gospel that Papias gave his judgment.

It is then without any support from tradition that Renan pictured, at the origin of the fourth gospel, John the son of Zebedee, still keeping his memory well enough to hand on the tradition of events, and a disciple making use of this canvas to embroider upon it doctrinal novelties.

His historical sense served him well in his judgment concerning the facts. "The historic groundwork of the fourth gospel is, to my mind, the life of Jesus as it was known among the immediate disciples of John. I must add that, in my opinion, this school was better acquainted with the exterior

[1] All the more because, according to Eusebius, Papias has made use of evidence drawn from the first Epistle of St. John. Renan speaks with contempt of Eusebius as "a bad judge in a question of criticism." But this is a question of fact.

circumstances of the life of the founder than the group whose remembrances constituted the synoptics."[1]

By maintaining this position a man exposed himself to the pity or ridicule of all German critics. Renan knew this, but he did not flinch, and he added to his thirteenth edition a special appendix giving his proofs. It is true that to abandon this position would have obliged him, not merely to go over again and correct his *Life of Jesus*, but entirely to re-write it, since it is built on the foundation of the fourth gospel. None the less, we are obliged to pay homage to the independence of his character and to his literary feeling. He could not make up his mind to rank the gospel according to St. John in the category of the Apocrypha, all utterly ignorant of history, and of geography, and caring nothing for concrete reality. Nor would he place it in the category of allegory, since allegory is self-revealing, and it is impossible to discover an allegorical meaning in a great number of the events it relates.

This discussion, numbering more than sixty pages, can still be read with advantage. We must always ask, he tells us, "What did this topographical detail matter to a sectary of Asia Minor or Alexandria?" Renan even takes the offensive rather roughly. "The really allegorical writings of the first centuries, the Apocalypse, the *Pastor* of Hermas, the *Pisté* (sic) *Sophia* are a very different style of thing. All this symbolism is at bottom allied to the myth

[1] p. 19.

theories of Strauss: both are expedients of an out at elbows theology, saving itself only by allegory, myth, or symbol." And this very pointed thrust, "In this case the partisans of an allegorical explanation play the part of the Alexandrians. It is they who, embarrassed by the fourth gospel, treat it as Philo treated Genesis, as all tradition, Jewish and Christian, has treated the Canticle of Canticles."[1]

This is quite definite, but if the fourth gospel contains an historical tradition superior to that of the synoptics, did its author know the synoptics, or did he not? A critic seems only to have his choice between these two contradictory hypotheses. Or again, he might not take either side. Renan hesitated. When he is arguing for the authenticity of the facts he is tempted to believe that John wanted to protest against the gospel stories that were in circulation and which did not give him a big enough place in the history of Christ. John the Apostle would even seem to have had a "system to explain" the composition of Mark's gospel.[2] Yet the final conclusion is: "There is nothing to prove that the compiler of the fourth gospel had, when writing, any of the synoptic gospels under his eyes."[3]

"Under his eyes" is not the point: the question is, did he *know* them? Renan does not dare to exclude this possibility. "If the author of the fourth gospel had read some document of the synoptic tradition, which is very possible, at least we must

[1] p. 509, French edition. [2] p. 19. [3] p. 18.

say that he had not got it under his eyes when he was writing."[1] Under his eyes again!

If John the Apostle had probably known the earlier writings how could they have been unknown by his disciple—a man doubtless of a more enquiring and educated mind? Renan, moreover, states as an established conclusion, "that the author of the fourth gospel, whoever he may have been, wrote to re-establish the authority of one of the apostles, to show that that apostle had played his part in circumstances in which the other histories made no mention of him, to prove that he knew things unknown to the other disciples."[2]

However, this point may stand, the comparison had to be undertaken between the synoptics and the fourth gospel. Commonly only the order of happenings is in question, and there is little that cannot be left to the free choice of the critic. One could not, for instance, reproach Renan for placing at the beginning of Our Lord's ministry the expulsion of the traffickers from the Temple: it is even the order preferred by Catholic exegesis. But it is self-contradiction to change one's view of the general character of the synoptics the better to defend the fourth evangelist. To uphold that his characters are not types, but historical beings of flesh and blood is very good, but this did not force Renan to continue, "It is the synoptics rather who have a turn for the idyllic and the legendary."[3] We know well enough who invented the idyll. And elsewhere,

[1] p. 530, French edition. [2] p. 536, French edition.
[3] p. 500, French edition.

when the fourth evangelist has swung down in his esteem, we shall be told that "he has not the naïveté, the absolute sincerity of Matthew and Mark."[1] Yet again, "The instinctive art which regulated the compilation of the synoptics, and often led them, in arranging the narrative, to study adaptability and effect."[2] The synthesis of these qualities, rather difficult to conciliate, is found in the statement that in the synoptics everything is "naïvely combined to produce its effect." One has no temptation to attribute naïveté to this sort of criticism. It is merely subtle to excess and it is carried away by prejudice in two very characteristic instances. These are the scenes of the Agony in the Garden and the institution of the Holy Eucharist. In the fourth gospel there is a passage which speaks of Our Lord as troubled—an anguish associated with the Saviour's glorification by a voice from on high (John xii, 27). With all the critics, from Strauss onwards, Renan says: "We cannot doubt that this is the parallel with the Agony in the Garden." After which he prefers the order of St. John, who places the episode several days before the passion. Why? This is his chief reason: "To accept the order of the synoptics one must suppose that Jesus knew with certainty the day on which he would die," and "historical criticism will always favour the less dramatic version."[3]

It would suffice to explain the Agony if Our Lord had a presentiment of His approaching death;

[1] p. 526, French edition. [2] p. 205.
[3] p. 578, French edition.

but even a distant view of supernatural certitude makes Renan lose his head. For otherwise he would have recognised that the "dramatic" quality in the Agony, that is to say, fear of death, and Our Lord's apparently useless prayer, were circumstances which the faithful would have been more tempted to conceal than to invent. No other critic has followed Renan. They fall over each other in declaring that the prepossessions of the fourth evangelist break out here openly, that he has cut out the humiliation of the episode and cast a halo round a moment of anguish. But whether, in fact, John is alluding to a separate trial through which Our Saviour's soul passed, or whether he has transposed some part of the scene of Gethsemane, already well known to the synoptists, we see his sincerity in throwing into relief the human nature of the Son of God. In any case there is no opportunity here for sacrificing a fact affirmed by the synoptic tradition, and against which the only argument is the silence of the fourth gospel.

The same reasoning holds good in the matter of the Institution of the Eucharist. Because the fourth gospel makes no allusion to it at the Last Supper we must cut out of history, not the Institution of the Eucharist (which happened several times instead of only once!) but the institution on the eve of the Passion. This omission constitutes "a feature of superiority" over the synoptics. I venture to say that we already know why. "To claim that Jesus reserved for the Thursday evening so important a ritual institution is to accept a sort of miracle, that is to suppose that he was certain he would die on the following day. Although we may believe that Jesus had his presentiments, we cannot, apart from the supernatural, accept such definite foresight."[1]

The supernatural! What a stumbling block! But, as a matter of fact, presentiments—and this time we *are* allowed to believe in presentiments—would be enough. St. Paul here corroborates the synoptic tradition,[2] and in the face of this argument what can John's silence signify? "The fourth evangelist, pre-occupied with Eucharistic ideas as he is, who relates the Last Supper with so much prolixity, connecting with it so many circumstances and discourses, does not mention this narrative. This is a proof that the sect whose tradition he represents did not regard the Eucharist as a peculiarity of the Last Supper."[3] Then why the details given by the synoptics and St. Paul? Because after the death of anyone dear "we concentrate into a few hours the memories of many years."[4] This *might* explain why the fourth gospel puts into Our Lord's mouth at this solemn hour so many sayings. It in no way explains how ancient tradition placed on the eve of His death a rite which expressly alludes to it and a discourse especially made for this event. Moreover, precisely because he had at the Last Supper so many discourses, the fourth evangelist may well have deemed it superfluous to reproduce the solemn words, the text of which was already

[1] p. 518, French edition.
[2] 1 Cor. xi, 23–5.
[3] p. 210.
[4] p. 209.

consecrated and held its place in the written tradition. Supposing that a critic of such criticism were to read a little farther: "As it was early believed that the repast in question took place on the day of the Passover, and was the Paschal feast, the idea naturally arose that the Eucharistic institution was established at this supreme moment."[1] This critic would surely feel forced to turn the proposition round: As they knew that the Eucharist was instituted at the Last Supper to replace the immolation of the lamb, the disciples came to give to this supper a paschal character—if it had not got it already![2] And what was this sect which did not regard the institution of the Eucharist as "a peculiarity of the Last Supper"? Were not the epistles of St. Paul read at Ephesus? But in that sect the ideas were quite different! For the fourth evangelist "the special rite of the Last Supper was the washing of feet."[3]

Anyhow, can we be certain from this that the washing of the feet itself was a historic event?

We should be startled if the preference for it were carried so far! and the washing of the feet practised by Jesus "on some occasions"[4] was also, with no greater reason, attributed to the eve of His death. The fourth gospel is only useful when it is silent or

[1] p. 209.

[2] On the previous page Renan says "It was not the ritual feast of the Passover, as was afterwards supposed owing to the error of a day in reckoning, but for the primitive Church this supper of the Thursday was the True Passover." (Translator's note.)

[3] p. 210.

[4] p. 210.

when it serves to give the lie to the others. In reality Renan's own conclusion—that "he was writing to prove his knowledge of things which the other disciples did not know"[1] (or rather had not related)—would be quite enough to explain both the silence of the fourth evangelist about the Eucharist and the addition of the washing of the feet. Had he wanted to contradict the rest on so important a point silence would not have been enough.

But, anyhow, let us be grateful to so hesitating a critic for having strongly distinguished the fourth gospel from works written only *ad probandum*. His wide erudition authorised the conclusion: "Nothing less resembles the biography of an æon; this is not the fashion in which India writes her lives of Krishna, and relates the incarnations of Vishnu. During the first centuries of our era we have an example of that kind of composition in the *Pisté Sophia* attributed to Valentine. Nothing in it is real; all is truly symbolic and ideal. I should say the same of the 'Gospel of Nicodemus' — an artificial composition built upon metaphor. Between our text and such embroiderings there is a gulf."[2]

These were hard sayings for the criticism then in fashion, and all Renan's disciples would doubtless have abandoned him had he not shown himself more accommodating on the question of the discourses. We, too, must acknowledge that the difficulty is

[1] p. 536, French edition.
[2] p. 489, French edition.

greater here, as the discourses are not on the same note as those of the synoptics. Is this a reason for saying that they are not really Christ's own sayings, representing His thought, His conversations with Nicodemus and the Samaritan woman, His arguments with the Jews, His outpourings with His disciples? Clearly not, for one disciple might as well have recalled different accents of the same Master as have placed His biography in a different framework. The rejection of the discourses comes badly from the very man who prefers this framework.

These discourses are, however, so evidently written in the style of the author of the gospel that in the particular case of a speech of John the Baptist, Catholic commentators have asked whether the whole discourse was the Baptist's or whether John the son of Zebedee had not taken his place without warning the reader (John ii, 31–36 cf. iii, 16–21). This objection of the unity of the style is both more and less important than it looks. More important, because the argument clearly proves the writer's intervention, less important because this intervention can usually be reduced to the style alone. We may go farther: Catholic critics, anxious to safeguard the inspiration of the holy scriptures in the strictest sense of the word, have not refused to recognise in the discourses of the fourth gospel a certain elaboration of Our Lord's thought. Here, too, the substance is distinguished from what is only a method of presenting it.

Renan has adopted a much more radical solution,

although, after his usual fashion, it is watered down by qualifications.

As we have already said, he uttered the big word, "heresy"—but without attaching much weight to the idea, since he did not attempt to offer the smallest proof. Later the reproach is softened: "Here we are in the midst of Philo's metaphysic, and almost that of the Gnostics."[1] At the same time these "discourses of Jesus, as reported by this man, claiming to be a witness, this intimate disciple, are false, often pointless, impossible."[2] They are not John's because "the Greek in which the gospel is written does not resemble the Palestinian Greek, which we know through the other books of the New Testament."[3] They are not Christ's. "It was not by pretentious tirades, heavy, badly written, and appealing little to the moral sense, that Jesus founded his divine work."[4] Lastly, they "are not historical," the proof of which is "their perfect harmony with the intellectual state of Asia Minor at the time when they were written."[5]

We cannot suppose that anyone was so irreverent to the learned member of the Institute as to try to find out what were the characteristics of the Palestinian Greek, which he flattered himself that he knew from the other books of the New Testament. Even since the re-awakening of the study of Hellenistic Greek it would be extremely embarrassing to have to define them. Nor are we much more

[1] p. 539, French edition.
[2] Id.
[3] p. 539, French edition.
[4] p. 15.
[5] p. 16.

advanced in our knowledge of the intellectual state of Asia Minor at this period. Renan cites Cerinthus, who only figures in Church history as the adversary refuted by St. John. This is all the Gnosticism contained in the fourth gospel! As to the metaphysic of Philo we venture to say that in this connexion it is a phrase empty of any meaning whatsoever.

In Philo, we find, if not a coherent metaphysical system, at least a continuous pretence of philosophy and an incontestable knowledge of the various systems which he is trying as best he may to amalgamate with each other and with the Bible. The fourth gospel opens with a sublime page, and contains many sublime sayings. But all that does not make metaphysics. By metaphysics we mean the study of ultimate causes by means of the light of reason. The fourth gospel pierces to the innermost Being of God, but by means of the revelation of God the Son. Certain modern writers desiring to avoid the word religion, replace it by the word metaphysics. A Christian and a freethinker have not, they say, the same metaphysical views. But Renan had no intention of using this journalistic terminology. The discourses of Jesus in the fourth gospel are the highest expression of revelation, without the least trace of syllogisms or categories or transcendent dialectic. Renan saw in them nothing useful to morality. This is astonishing, for he would still have claimed seriously what he finished by saying in jest, that morality and religion were inseparable. John's morality is certainly built upon religious faith, but that faith leads to action. Gnosticism was refuted in advance by a single saying from the fourth gospel, "He that doeth truth cometh to the light."[1] And all the discourses strike this note. They speak much of truth, of light, and of love. But to love is to fulfil the commandments.[2]

That the discourses are badly written is only a question of style, not of authenticity, and Renan himself admits it. "This by no means implies," he says, "that there are not in the discourses of John some admirable gleams, some traits which truly come from Jesus."[3] Among these traits are the words spoken to the woman of Samaria about "the pure worship of all ages, of all lands."[4] If this saying is authentic, however far removed from the Master's usual way of speaking, it is hard to see why so many other sayings are judged with such severity.

We are offered an analogy about these sayings. "They are, so to speak, the variations of a musician improvising on a given theme. The theme is not without some authenticity, but in the execution the imagination of the artist has given itself full scope."[5] Very well—but everything depends upon the "given

[1] John iii, 21.
[2] John xiv, 21.
[3] p. 15.
[4] p. 140. This saying could not, however, be left standing without attenuation and explanation. Elsewhere we read (p. 494, French edition): "If Jesus never uttered this divine saying it no less belongs to him. Without him it could not have been spoken." Now we are all in agreement!
[5] p. 16.

theme." If this theme be, as is abundantly evident, the incarnation and the mission of the Son of God we might, perhaps, reach an agreement about the utterance of "variations" in the musical sense. . . . But this is not what Renan means, and he ends by rejecting the authenticity of the theme.

He has, of course, foreseen the objection: why give so much credit to the fourth gospel over the facts, and so little over the doctrines? Is not the same tradition which has faithfully reported the facts worthy of belief when it records the Master's teaching? He replies by two comparisons of very unequal worth. "The discourses which Sallust and Livy put into their histories are undoubtedly fictitious. Are we to conclude from this that the foundation of these histories is equally fictitious?"[1] But these discourses are fragments of pageantry, set pieces of eloquence, bearing no resemblance to the words of Jesus which are mingled with His actions and improperly enough labelled discourses. The "discourses" most attacked are the dialogues with the Jews, because in them Our Lord speaks of His divinity. Renan was, therefore, much nearer a true comparison when he used that of Xenophon and Plato, both interpreters of Socrates. He sacrifices Plato almost completely. "In order to describe the Socratic teaching, should we follow the 'dialogues' of Plato or the 'conversations' of Xenophon? Doubt in this respect is not possible; everyone chooses the 'conversations,' and not the 'dialogues.'

[1] p. 520, French edition.

Does Plato, however, teach us nothing about Socrates? Would it be good criticism, in writing the biography of the latter, to neglect the 'dialogues'? Who would venture to maintain this?"[1]

I know neither what was the erudite view at the time Renan was writing nor what it is to-day, but it is enough to have read the "conversations" and the "dialogues" to be able to assert that the complete Socrates is not to be found in Xenophon. The aptitude for philosophy of this honourable cavalry officer was mediocre enough, and his Socrates never rises above a straightforward and mediocre intellectual banality. Who could believe that Plato would have fallen under the charm of the man if there had been no more in him than that? Would he have put at the service of a mere mouthpiece of good sense his own penetrating dialectic, his acute irony, his divine ideas? Without over-stressing the importance of a comparison we may well deduce from this one that there is more to be drawn from the fourth gospel than biographical details.

Moreover is fidelity in biographical details to be found apart from historical truth? It may be that such a picture of Napoleon, as was drawn by Taine, does not, in spite of so many accurate features, give as complete a portrait as some sketch of a few lines. Yet, unless the aspect of the person sketched is an invention the authentic details must fit in somewhere in the complete physiognomy. And we must allow

[1] p. 19.

something for Renan's domination by his theory. The fourth gospel does not really show either so much art or so much malice. It is, therefore, impossible to say with Renan that if the material information given by the fourth gospel is "more accurate than that of the synoptics the historical colouring is much less so."[1] The Johannine tradition, as evaluated by Renan, goes back directly, or indirectly to an eye-witness. Is it likely to have retained the accurate remembrance of so many minor incidents,[2] and to have forgotten the "general physiognomy" (if it may be so described) of an adored Master?

As M. Wallon has wisely said: "Dr. Strauss treats the evangelists as he would copyists who are reproducing the single picture of the same painter. They are in reality themselves painters, and their pictures vary because their subjects are in motion."[3]

Renan is right when he refuses to accept the dilemma of the German rationalists—either hold purely and simply to the events and the order of John as an eye-witness, or else see in the fourth gospel nothing but the theological creation of a group of Christians at Ephesus. Why should not John, too, have arranged the facts and the discourses without always following a strict chronology? And if the French savant was so much dominated by his theory that he exaggerated the contrast

[1] p. 537, French edition.

[2] For Renan keeps many of these although rejecting "traits which can have no real value," for example: i, 40; ii, 6; iv, 52; v, 5, 9; vi, 9, 19; xxi, 11.

[3] *De la Croyance due à l'Evangile*, Second edition, Part II, chapter VI.

between the facts and the discourses, he did not, take it all in all, lack either historical discernment or courage in making such a constant use of the fourth gospel. "Everyone who sets himself to write the life of Jesus without any predetermined theory as to the relative value of the gospels, letting himself be guided solely by the sentiment of the subject, will be led, in numerous instances, to prefer the narration of John to that of the synoptics. The last months of the life of Jesus, especially, are explained by John alone; a number of the features of the Passion, unintelligible in the synoptics, resume both probability and possibility in the narrative of the fourth gospel."[1]

Yet he abstained from any discussion on the order of Mark, the question of Luke's dependence on Mark and the relation of Matthew with the two others—all questions already under discussion in 1863, and from 1868 on he never changed a line of his certainly too summary sketch of the composition of the gospels. He had taken up his final position.

Renan merits praise for realising the "gulf" which separates the canonical from the apocryphal gospels, which "are insipid and puerile amplifications."[2] Rightly, too, he does not put into this category the gospel according to the Hebrews, nor the gospel according to the Egyptians. But, strangely enough, he ranges these latter in one group with "the Gospels styled those of Justin, Marcion and Tatian."[3] The first two were, we are told, the

[1] p. 18. [2] p. 22. [3] p. 23.

gospel of the Eibonites—that is to say of the little Christian communities of Batanea. But this cannot be the case with the Gospel according to the Egyptians. It is, on the other hand, very accurate to say that "these gospels are inferior, as critical authorities, to the compilation of Matthew's gospel, which we now possess."[1] Yet once more this judgment does not agree with what is said elsewhere about the "simple and sweet Christian families of Batanea, among whom the collection of Λόγια was formed,"[2] all the more as, in yet another place we find that the sayings were "collected by Matthew."[3] These "little companies" of Batanea, very pure, very honest, offer the most perfect contrast with the tradition of the fourth gospel, for they "might at the same time have preserved accurately the note of the Master's voice, and be very badly informed on the biographical facts by which they set little store."[4] The contrast is entertaining between this little conservative world, indifferent to facts, and the Ephesian sect, a school of theological development, but clinging to facts and to chronology. We must remember that the communities of Batanea could have no special authority unless they represented the Christians of Jerusalem who left the holy city a little before the year 70. But the "Logia" were then in existence! All, therefore, that can be attributed to these very pure little companies is the remodelling of a first gospel already judged inferior to our canonical Matthew.

[1] p. 23.
[2] p. 502, French edition.
[3] p. 9.
[4] p. 502, French edition.

Renan has given no opinion on the value of Josephus, but it obtrudes constantly in his writing. Josephus is the touchstone of the truth of the gospels, and the sovereign criterion in topographical discussions—even in his descriptions, the exaggerations of which are obvious, and which are so often inaccurate.[1] Yet as a critic Renan has carefully noted the "varnish of banality,"[2] which effaces in Josephus anything to do with Messianic beliefs and which "makes all the heads of Jewish sects resemble professors of morality or Stoics."

The disciple of Pallas Athene could not disguise his repugnance for the composition of the Talmud. Yet he attributes to it great authority. According to him the dates matter little, whatever those may think who are accustomed to attribute value to a document only for the period at which it was written. But "such scruples would here be out of place. The teaching of the Jews from the Ashmonean epoch, down to the second century, was principally oral. We must not judge of this state of intelligence by the habits of an age of much writing."[3] This is doubtless true: we are quite agreed about it, and only ask that it may be remembered *à propos* to the gospels. For if the Mishna, drawn up towards the year 200 A.D., if the Talmuds of Jerusalem and

[1] p. 21, Luke "commits errors in . . . topography." Compare Luke xxiv, 13 to Jos. vii, vi, 6. note to Dindorf ed. It is the difficult question of Emmaus which Renan evidently has not studied closely. Cf. on the identity of Capharnaüm with Tell Hum the conjecture supported by Josephus, p. 147, note, French edition.

[2] p. 108, note, French edition.

[3] p. 6.

Babylon, whose *gemara* or complement to the Mishna was only drawn up towards the year 500, faithfully reproduce the sayings of Rabbis anterior to the Christian era, we may thereby be re-assured about the preservation of the words of Christ.

Renan profited then by the rabbinical literature to learn the ideas of the masters of old, and he even advanced the theory that "one might recompose . . . the morality of the gospels . . . almost entirely by the aid of older maxims."[1] But he had too much intelligence—or simply enough intelligence—not to attempt to carry out a detailed parallel. He would not have succeeded judging by the only example he gives. "As to justice he (Christ) was content with repeating the well-known axiom—'Do not do to others what ye would not that they should do to you.'"[2]

The distortion is glaring, for the passages referred to in a note, Matt. vii, 12; Luke vi, 31, contain the precept in the positive form, making a much more searching demand, to do to others what you would wish them to do to you! Renan himself says: "It is neither the ancient Law nor the Talmud which has conquered and changed the world."[3]

[1] p. 72, We need not trouble to reconcile this appreciation with another which we find on p. 128. "The science of the Jewish doctor, of the *sofer* or scribe, was purely barbarous, unmitigatedly absurd, and denuded of all moral element." And in a note to the French edition "We can judge what it was from the Talmud, an echo of the Jewish teaching of the period."

[2] p. 86, French edition. This is given in the *Everyman* Translation, p. 72, as "Whatsoever you would that men should do to you, do ye even so to them."!

[3] p. 72.

But to mark the superiority of the Gospels was it enough to speak of an accent full of unction and of the poetry of the teaching which made men love it? It would be enough, only were this unction the "spiritalis unctio" of the Holy Ghost, this poetry the Incarnation of the Word of God.

III

The Historical Method

Despite his theories on the composition of the gospels and on their inter-relations Renan might still have written history. Goethe has said that the past is a book sealed with seven seals[1], and this is true for everybody. When he adds that the "spirit" of the period is at bottom the personal outlook of those through whom the period is reflected, he is stating the law that all history is to a certain degree an interpretation. Nevertheless, there are two very different fashions of interpreting the past. The critic must not certainly be blinded by a cult of written records, and the historian must make every effort to paint a picture of bygone events, giving to them a countenance and not merely isolated and lifeless features. But he must be so absorbed in his work as to lose sight of himself, lest the mirror of the ages should merely reflect his own picture. In other words one sort of history is realist, objective, and impersonal, in the other sort the author is seen in every line with his own outlook on life, his passions, and his prejudices. Strangely enough Brunetière[2] placed Renan in the former category, because he

[1] *Faust*, I, 223. [2] *Le xixe Siecle.*

wrote at a time of reaction against Romanticism and individualism, and because he wrote in scientific jargon. M. Séailles was much more penetrating; "*The History of the Origins of Christianity* is written to confirm Renan's favourite theories."[1] The theories are certainly to be found, but we must look behind them, and what appears behind them is the talent and even the person of the author. And why should we not openly admit that this is what gives the book its charm, and what at the same time fills believers with a repulsion which they do not feel in the same degree in reading more violent attacks. The charm of the book cannot fail to seduce some good people, for Renan's mind seems very frank, very flexible, able to understand everything, inclined to admire all that is admirable, free from all prejudice, but respectful, and full of pious unction, towards all that is beautiful and noble. But when we understand the smiling irony underneath this unction, the evil insinuations defacing this respect, the passion raging beneath this apparent serenity, and the prejudice throughout, we suffer at seeing the whole story, and even the adorable Face of Jesus, darkened by the shadow of this man, who still dares to call Him his friend. M. Séailles has not exaggerated in pointing out that Renan "desired that Jesus should reflect the image of himself, and in this image he took immense delight."[2] Did he not admit this in attributing to Jesus—I warn the reader that it is a blasphemy—the disillusioned smile of the mandarin. "The man of the world is unknown to us who lacks

[1] *Ernest Renan*, p. 131. [2] Id., p. 137.

a touch of the sceptic. . . . While Jesus possessed in the highest degree that which we look upon as the essential quality of a person of distinction, I mean the gift of smiling over his own work, of being superior to it, of not letting himself become obsessed by it, Paul was not free from the defect which shocks us in sectaries: he carried his faith heavily."[1]

But let us look a little closer.

Let us, 'with the nineteenth century apologists', distinguish between the two aspects of the gospels. The Catholic, as a part of his faith, venerates them as inspired documents. Hence he cannot treat them as ordinary books. But, precisely because he has confidence in their truth as holy books, he is not alarmed at their being subjected to a critical examination. It is certainly the fact that unbelieving critics approach their study without the slightest respect for the divine words that are in them. We are convinced that this study may be useful, because we are convinced that the gospels prove to every noble soul and upright mind the divine mission of Jesus Christ. We ask only that the conditions of a historical study should be adhered to. Under these circumstances there is no ground for astonishment if a man does not draw from a simple examination of the gospels all the conclusions that flow from their character as inspired documents. Whatever early Protestantism may have said, this character of Inspiration is not overwhelmingly apparent from the text, even in an examination undertaken with the grace of the Holy Spirit.

[1] *L'Antichrist*, p. 111.

In the same way we cannot demand of the critic to establish in the first place harmony between the different texts, and to declare them free from all error. Weighing them as human documents he is convinced beforehand that they contain error like all other documents, and he will treat them as such, trying to separate error and truth according to the value of the documents themselves. It is our task to defend them, but before undertaking it we must protect ourselves as it were, and provisionally, behind "the rules of the game."

A few errors of detail, as they may well appear at first sight, a few apparent contradictions, of which the certain solution cannot be found, do not authorise anyone to reject the value of the documents on points where their witness is overwhelming.

These obvious truths had to be repeated because Renan never drew the distinction. "If there were," he said, "in Tacitus, or in Polybius, errors as definite as those which Luke commits *à propos* of Quirinius and of Theudas, we should say that Tacitus and Polybius had been mistaken."[1] For the explanation of these cases reference may be had to scriptural commentaries,[2] and the theologians will give them due weight, but still if Tacitus and Polybius made mistakes, a thing which might happen even to Thucydides, it would not be thereby concluded that their works were legendary. And it will be admitted that if Renan found no other historical mistakes in

[1] p. vii, French edition.

[2] On the Census of Quirinius, cf. *Revue Biblique*, 1913. Theudas appears only in the speech of Gamaliel (Acts v, 36).

the third gospel and in the Acts, Luke would still appear to be a pretty good historian. Of course, as theologians, we have to prove that the facts alleged are not incompatible with the Catholic idea of inspiration, but obliged as we often are to be satisfied with probable solutions, we can scarcely be astonished if critics maintain other solutions which appear to them more probable. It would be to overweight the examination of such a work as the *Life of Jesus* to discuss all the points on which Renan has rejected the testimony of the gospels. The general question only shall be put: What did he think of them as historical documents? What credit did he accord to them?

We already know that he regarded them as in great part legendary, that is to say, filled with untrue stories, for they continually speak of miracles, and no miracle has ever happened. It could not be put more clearly: "It is not because it has in the first place been demonstrated that the evangelists are not deserving of absolute faith that I reject the miracles they relate. It is because they relate miracles, that I say 'the gospels are legends.' They may contain history, but certainly not everything in them is historical."[1]

But, after all, this is begging the question. Elsewhere Renan has vigorously denied his right to reason on this point as a philosopher, firmly declaring that he is only a historian. He rejects miracles because "nobody has ever seen one," and the evangelists say they have seen them (St. John), or that the people they have consulted have seen them

[1] p. vi, French edition.

(St. Luke). Or again, they relate them without mention of themselves, but with the absolute conviction that supernatural events have been accomplished in broad daylight and in the presence of irrefutable witnesses (St. Matthew and St. Mark). He could not then avoid giving judgment on the value of the evangelists as witnesses.

They are not as we know historians in the ordinary sense, for they are not relating a series of events of the political or military order, with careful observation of the circumstances of time and place. And it may be said that we know more from Thucydides of what happened at Athens during the first years of the Peloponnesian war, than we know of what happened in Judea under Pontius Pilate. But that is not the question either. The evangelists concentrated on a single figure, one may almost say on the religious actions of that figure—Christ's preaching of the Kingdom of God, which showed him to be the Messiah, and brought Him to his death. Do we know Pericles, or Nicias, or Alcibiades better than we know Jesus? Obviously that depends on the worth of the evangelists as witnesses of His Life.

This is how Renan looked at it. "Let us suppose that, ten or twelve years ago, three or four old soldiers of the Empire had each undertaken to write the life of Napoleon from memory. It is clear that their narratives would contain numerous errors, and great discordances. One of them would place Wagram before Marengo; another would write without hesitation that Napoleon drove the Government of Robespierre from the Tuileries; a third would omit expeditions of the highest importance. But one thing would certainly result with a great degree of truthfulness from these simple recitals, and that is the character of the hero, the impression which he made round him. In this sense such popular narratives would be worth more than a formal and official history. We may say as much of the gospels."[1]

The whole of this parallel is a false one. Renan is speaking of soldiers, meaning old veterans—soldiers drawn from the people. How could they have known the hero whom they had never seen close by? At the very utmost they could only have been the echo of a legend, the legend of the "Petit Caporal," familiar with his soldiers. What would be most lacking in these stories would be precisely the true character of the hero, and I doubt whether Taine or Vandal consulted such witnesses to sound the depths of Bonaparte's soul. They would scarcely have retained a glimmering reflection from his aureole. And where are the old soldiers who have claimed to write the life of Napoleon from their memories? It is true that stories of this sort of veteran have been published relating such and such a campaign. But in vain would one look amongst them for a complete biography of the General. On the other hand many details appear to be absolutely accurate; these good people relate what they have seen: for Napoleon crossed their horizon in a blaze of glory, and if he drew near them they were dazzled.

[1] p. 23.

The evangelists, on the other hand, record, whether at first or second hand, the recollections of the apostles themselves. This capital point is admitted by Renan, but here he should have recalled the Eastern way of life. No intimacy in our countries with their severe climate and the modern fashion of life, in which each man lives in his own house, can give any idea of the life in common led by Jesus and His disciples, living under the blue sky, often sleeping beneath the stars, partaking in a boat or in the fields, of a meal cooked at a fire provided there and then, round which they all sat. The conversation was continuous save when the Master retired for prayer, a constant exchange of question and answer, a gradual breaking down of prejudices as their minds were opened, whose hearts had been already won. The picture of our Lord was not presented to them finished and complete, already famous; it was formed gradually in the souls of men of good will, who, however, found themselves in frequent opposition to a mind so unlike their own! It is these disciples of several years, these friends, slowly imbued with a doctrine which they were afterwards to preach, whom Renan compares with the nameless crowd of soldiers whom Napoleon led in his battles! There is a real analogy only on one point: the victories of Napoleon won the enthusiasm of the faithful veterans; the miracles of Christ won the belief of his disciples.

Yet Renan complained, with his habitual tone of sweetness at being accused of scepticism. "Far from being accused of scepticism I should be counted among the moderate critics, because, instead of rejecting *en bloc* documents which are weakened by so much alloy, I try to extract something of history from them by delicate approximations."[1] And certainly, compared to Strauss—not to speak of Bruno Bauer—Renan was a moderate historian, more moderate, indeed, then those liberal Protestants who usually write with a total disregard of the fourth gospel. But precisely because they pretended to a stricter selection of documents, they thought themselves more certain of getting near the truth of history. They certainly achieved more easily a portrait not lacking in a certain psychological unity. The documents were fewer, but they had to be regarded. The historian had no longer the right to break away from them. It was sufficient for him to have sorted them at his own pleasure.

Less arbitrary as a critic, and thus making use of more extensive materials, Renan is determined to use them after his own fashion. It cannot be said that he is dishonest in this, since he proclaimed it openly, but he is certainly wanting in accuracy. Extremely anxious not to give himself away to the sceptics, yet desirous to extract from such a beautiful legend a story pleasant to read, he invites us to savour the art of his " delicate approximations " after having forbidden us to believe in them.

In 1863, when Renan's *Life of Jesus* appeared, the reaction against Strauss' *Life of Jesus* had ended in a history rebuilt out of the ruins that had been

[1] p. v. French edition.

accumulated. To this Strauss himself lent a hand by writing in 1864 his *Life of Jesus for the German People.* Renan observed moderately, "Strauss supposes the individuality of Jesus to be more effaced for us than it probably is in fact."[1]

Strauss had dowered "the community" with all the genius which he denied to its Master. Renan realized that in doing this he would lose his hero, and what is more to the point, his subject. He had been for a moment tempted towards the same mistake, and if he does not confess it in great detail, at least his repentance expresses his French common sense. "When I first conceived the idea of a history of the origin of Christianity, what I wished to write was, in fact, a history of doctrines, in which men and their actions would have hardly had a place. Jesus would scarcely have been named; I should have endeavoured to show how the ideas which have grown under His Name took root and covered the world. But I have learned since that history is not a simple game of abstractions; that men are more than doctrines. It was not a certain theory on justification and redemption which brought about the Reformation; it was Luther and Calvin. Parseeism, Hellenism, Judaism, might have been able to have combined under every form; the doctrines of the Resurrection and of the Word might have developed themselves during ages without producing this grand, unique, and fruitful fact called Christianity. This fact is the work of Jesus, of St. Paul, of St. John."[2]

[1] p. xxxviii, note, French edition. [2] pp. 28, 29.

This is what the school of Comparative Religions desires to make us doubt afresh. Round about 1863 Germany did not, however, dream of toning down Christ's human action.

But Renan would not have been Renan if he had not sneered slightly in making this declaration. He did not want to be taken for a simple believer; he comes back, therefore, almost to the angle from which Strauss first wrote. What can be known for certain about Jesus? "He existed. He was born at Nazareth in Galilee. He preached attractively, and left his sayings profoundly imprinted in the memory of his disciples. The two chief of his disciples were Cephas and John the son of Zebedee. He excited the hatred of the orthodox Jews, who succeeded in getting him put to death under Pontius Pilate, at that time Procurator of Judea. He was crucified outside the city gate. People believed afterwards that he had risen again. . . Beyond this, doubt is permissible."[1] And this permissible doubt is not merely about unimportant points. "Did he consider himself the Messiah? Did he imagine that he worked miracles? Were they attributed to him during his lifetime? What was his moral character, etc."[2]

The life of Jesus was then contained in a few lines, and could have been written "even if the gospels did not exist or were untruthful,"[3] but a Renan would not have taken great pleasure in it. Having taken this precaution against the critics,

[1] p. xvi, French edition. [2] p. xvi, French edition.
[3] p. xvi, French edition.

or perhaps given this satisfaction to his own sovereign right of facing both ways, he made up his mind to write a true history, quite as certain on the whole as any other, and he *does* lean on the gospels, for he is careful to note the points on which he rejects their authority. From what source did his self-confidence flow?

First of all from his travels in the East. This, we might call the great lure which caught hold of an easily contented public. Having viewed the East, more especially Palestine, with the eyes of a critic, a man knows exactly what the Supernatural is worth, and how it imposed upon the easy credulity of the West. Renan expresses himself more elegantly and speaks seriously of a revelation. "To the perusal of documentary evidences I have been able to add an important source of information—the sight of the place where the events occurred. The scientific mission, having for its object the exploration of ancient Phœnicia, which I directed in 1860 and 1861, led me to reside on the frontier of Galilee, and to travel there frequently. I have travelled in all directions the country of the Gospels; I have visited Jerusalem, Hebron, and Samaria; scarcely any important locality of the history of Jesus has escaped me. All this history, which at a distance seems to float in the clouds of an unreal world, thus took a form, a solidity, which astonished me. The striking agreements of the texts with the places, the marvellous harmony of the Gospel ideal with the country which served it as a framework, were like a revelation to me. I had before my eyes a fifth

Gospel, torn, but still legible, and henceforward, through the recitals of Matthew and Mark, in place of an abstract being, whose existence might have been doubted, I saw, living and moving, an admirable human figure."[1]

An imprudent apologist would be tempted to translate this by saying "knowledge of the East of to-day confirms the Bible." But such a translation would not be in accord with the hidden meaning of the words, nor, above all, with the application of them, which alone gives them a definite meaning.

What, then, did Renan learn in the East which was for him a revelation, or a fifth gospel?

It is certainly a fact that in coming into contact with places and monuments history gathers strength, and becomes a living reality, where the flight of the unaided imagination has carried it too near the clouds. The agreement, in particular, of topography with the documents establishes their truth on an important point. Where certain details could not have been imagined or known from a distance we have proof that the authors have either been eye-witnesses or in close touch with tradition. Renan did not overburden himself with these detailed studies. It would be pedantry to reproach him for this, only his assertion was so very definite! His attempts to discover traces of ancient sites amount to very little, and were never successful. The identity of Capernaum and Tell Hum appears to him more than doubtful,[2] although there were good reasons in its support even before the recent discovery of

[1] pp. 27–8. [2] pp. 97–8.

a splendid synagogue. On the other hand, to consider Joutta to be that town of Juda of which Luke speaks is only an identification copied in his library from Robinson.[1] As Renan visited Hebron, he ought not to place the region where John baptized near Ramat-el-Khalil.[2] Water is rare at this part of the plateau of Hebron, and the name Ainon should have led him to accept the opinion of St. Jerome, who placed Salim in the valley of the Jordan, south of Beisan. It is as a philologist that he considered the names of Ainon and Sichar to carry weight in favour of the authenticity (as he understood the term!) of the fourth gospel.[3] *Apropos* to this last name he says truly, "Only a Jew of Palestine, who had often passed by the entry into the valley of Sichem could have written," the verses, 3 to 6, of John iv. But why add "verses 5 and 6 are inaccurate"?[4] We can still write to-day, "The site of Dalmanutha is quite unknown."[5] But it was not just to conclude from this fact that "the stories common to Matthew and Mark show copyists' errors, witnessing to a very slight knowledge of Palestine."[6] For, after all, first one swallow does not make a summer, secondly, *Magadan*

[1] p. 99, French edition.

[2] p. 79.

[3] pp. 492–3, French edition.

[4] In point of fact the well of the Samaritan woman is certainly Bir Jakoub. The Greeks, who have recently acquired it, have cleaned it out, and it has been found to be more than one hundred feet in depth. *Puteus altus est* (John iv, 11), a feature which Renan would not have failed to allege in favour of the fourth gospel.

[5] p. 146, French edition.

[6] p. 146, French edition.

(Mark xv, 39) cannot be an alteration of Dalmanutha (Mark viii, 10), and, finally, Dalmanutha may, on the other hand, be itself a copyist's error.[1] Again Renan should have been more assertive in finding Chorazin in the ruins of Kersah, and less sure about Gergesa, which he places at Koursi, an impossible situation for the episode of the pigs and the man possessed by a legion of devils.[2]

Once more, it is not my intention to discuss Renan's topography, which was as good as anyone else's at the time at which he wrote, but merely to point out that he did not, in reality, attach much importance to it. He followed Thompson or Robinson. It is not from this that light came to him. Neither did his revelation come from what the Germans call vaguely archæology, uniting in that one word the knowledge of customs and of monuments. The only ancient monuments in Galilee are the Synagogues, which Renan rightly dates as second or third century after Jesus Christ, so he certainly did not make use of them to elucidate the documents. He is silent, too, about many interesting details, such as the buildings of Galilee, the customs of the fishermen, the nets they use, the winds that blow on the lake. There is no comparison given which can help us to understand how a stone could be rolled away to open the entrance into a tomb. And is it not contrary to

[1] Cf. p. 146, note 3, French edition and the commentary of St. Mark on this place.

[2] pp. 146, 151, French edition.

the meaning to translate as ante-chamber[1] the court where Peter was warming himself with the servants of the High Priests?[2] The Pretorium is placed near the Temple, perhaps through an excessive docility towards tradition. The temple—the cardinal point of Palestinian archæology—is neither explained nor described. Golgotha may be placed to the north-west, or to the east, or wherever else you like, rather than on the spot chosen by Constantine.[3] None of this is of much interest to the philosophic historian; once more, whence came his light?

First of all, he tells us, from the scenery, which he described soberly as an artist. This M. Schweitzer could not understand. It remained an enigma to him that French art, so apt in painting to understand nature in all its admirable reality, in poetry should see it only through the medium of personal impressions, in an artificial manner, and, as he calls it, lyrico-sentimentally.[4] Renan, like Lamartine, like Loti, would have been ready to make any stage effects as a frame for his lyrical themes.

To these there must be added Chateaubriand, and the group becomes big enough to defend itself. Let us put painting aside rather than repeat once more Amiel's hackneyed saying, "A landscape is a state of the soul." How can the writer give life to a picture without mingling with his description of places the feelings inspired in him by their beauty and by their memories: and where the impression felt harmonises with that which those of old—Christ

[1] p. 214.
[2] John xviii, 15.
[3] p. 429, French edition.
[4] Geschichte der Leben-Jesu-Forsehung, p. 181.

Himself, for instance—must have felt, what is lacking to the charm of the picture? With mere words the writer would be too inferior to the painter in rendering line and colour, but neither line nor colour exists without eyes, and the human mind has the right to see in nature more than nature could offer apart from it. " Ain-el-Heramie, the last halting-place, is a charming and melancholy spot, and few impressions equal that experienced on camping there for the night. The valley is narrow and sombre, and a dark stream issues from the rock, full of tombs, which forms its banks. It is, I think, the 'valley of tears,' or of dropping waters, which is described as one of the stations on the way in the delightful eighty-fourth Psalm, and which became the emblem of life for the sad and sweet mysticism of the Middle Ages. Early the next day they would be at Jerusalem ; such an expectation now sustains the caravan, rendering the night short and slumber light."[1]

You will admit that, soothed by this rhythm, one does not dream of cross-questioning the author. But did Christ really travel in a caravan and sleep under a tent?—for otherwise He must have avoided this desert region. And is it really valley of tears that the psalmist means or valley of balsam trees, or even " very dry place "? Such are the objections that Wagner's *famulus* would have made to Faust. But who would have the courage to break the spell which likens the whole world, this valley of tears, to the horizon of a valley where Jesus slept the eve of his entry into Jerusalem !

[1] pp. 65–6.

We must, however, sometimes take our choice between poetry and criticism. The scenery does not always give us all Renan has attributed to it. We read again, "The environs, moreover, are charming; and no place in the world was so well adapted for dreams of perfect happiness. Even in our times Nazareth is still a delightful abode, the only place, perhaps, in Palestine in which the mind feels itself relieved from the burden which oppresses it in this unequalled desolation."[1]

Can you believe it? Sancho Panza would not have seen all these beautiful things, and, sheltering myself behind him and his good sense, I am inclined to ask whether the smiling aspect of Nazareth, in common with that of several other villages, does not arise from the fact that their population has remained Christian? As to the surroundings, it is always the same trees and the same hills, as our Sancho would say, and many another corner of Galilee is equally favourable for all sorts of dreams. And as to these dreams of absolute happiness, it is strange, is it not, that they were born in Jerusalem? Yet Jerusalem and Judea form the dark shadow beside this light, "The dreariness of Judea beyond, parched as by a scorching wind of desolation and death."[2]

Was it not really dried up by the wind which blew from the over-heated banks of the Dead Sea, and was not the desert of Judea enough to make Judea melancholy without these "desolations"?

[1] p. 44. And on p. 64, "In no country in the world do the mountains spread themselves out with more harmony (?) or inspire higher thoughts." (!!!)

[2] p. 45.

Was the whole of Judea absorbed by religious metaphysic, and are not the surroundings of Hebron as enchanting as those of Nazareth? Moreover, is it not in the desert that one longs for living waters! and are we to be surprised if apocalpytic dreams of absolute happiness took their rise from melancholy Judea like to a triumph over death?

Should landscapes, whether sad or cheerful, be translated into theories? Surely all this is a little childish.

Yet Renan treats this theme with all seriousness, and there is an element which gives it a certain speciousness. In Galilee the sky was clement, the shadows fresh, and life easy. Only in such a country as this could Jesus have preached detachment from the things of earth, confidence in Providence, a life without care, a veritable defiance of the economic laws which govern less favoured countries. No one, indeed, denies that the Saviour took His images, comparisons, and parables from the soil whereon He dwelt, from the customs of His fellow countrymen, from a sky which was rose-coloured both morning and eve. Yet we must remember that Galilee had suggested to no one else the counsels of perfection, and that this evangelic ideal of perfection has been able to be transplanted into rougher climates. That is because these counsels came from the soul of the Saviour, and from the burning charity which He had for His Father and for men, a charity which from the first day when he preached to them the Kingdom of God took the form of a call to penitence. Renan, as a superior artist, took great delight in the exquisite beauty of a Springtime in Galilee. He tasted of nature at the time when she appears most sweet to man among the flowering laurels, and on the still waters of the lake; he felt her invitation to joy, and took his inspiration therefrom. It is this which makes him say: "The whole history of infant Christianity has become in this manner a delightful pastoral."[1]

Such was the new revelation which extended to the character of the inhabitants of two countries as different from each other as light and darkness, joy and melancholy: Galilee and Judea. Thus we know why Jesus preached after a different manner from John: "Leave the austere Baptist in his desert of Judea to preach penitence, to inveigh without ceasing, and to live on locusts in the company of jackals. Why should the companions of the bridegroom fast while the bridegroom is with them? Joy will be a part of the Kingdom of God."[2]

Yet there are different kinds of joy. This revelation is able to distinguish between them. "This contented and easily satisfied life was not like the gross materialism of our peasantry, the coarse pleasures of agricultural Normandy, or the heavy mirth of the Flemish. It spiritualised itself in ethereal dreams—in a kind of poetic mysticism, blending heaven and earth."[3]

Here, indeed, we have that really distinguished joy, which Renan was able to approve, at least at the time when he was so strongly opposed to

[1] p. 65. [2] pp. 64–5. [3] p. 64.

Béranger and his epicurean songs. . . . It is most attractive, but that does not mean it is to be taken seriously. Here is his argument based on the monuments: "From the ruins which remain of its ancient splendour we can trace an agricultural people, no way gifted in art, caring little for luxury, indifferent to the beauties of form, and exclusively idealistic."[1]

These ruins are doubtless the *débris* of canals, which suggest to the enlightened archæologist an agricultural people. That their artistic capacity was slight may be said of all the Jews. The Galileans were then indifferent to beauty of form, and, being peasants or fishermen they could hardly have afforded the expense of luxuries even if they desired them. Certainly in Galilee, as elsewhere, the rich sought their own ease and comfort. Renan fails to show how these ruins prove the exclusive idealism of this people.[2] It is certainly by no means evident in the Gospels, even if we look for it in the Disciples of Jesus. These have, along with aspirations, which are very practical and rather ordinary, a deep sense of the rights of God which always has an elevating effect upon souls; but was not this sense even more powerful in Jerusalem?

Lacking monuments, Renan might surely have examined Josephus more closely on the true character of the Galileans. "The Galileans were held to be energetic, brave, laborious."[3] But doubtless

[1] p. 64.
[2] By contrast presumably with the people of Judea?
[3] Jos. B. J. III, III 2.

his idyll would have fled away at the contact with these men of energetic nature, very laborious, very anxious about their own well-being even when most carried away by their religious dreams. For their religion itself bore a strong impress of national spirit, and of the hope of a happiness, earthly and even planted in the soil. Is it then from what he saw in the country with his own eyes that Renan manufactured his chimerical Galileans? In that case what like are the Galileans of to-day? The people of Nazareth[1] have more resemblance to those of Bethlehem—in Judea! —than to the poor creatures burnt and blackened by the sun, at the same time lazy, yet occasionally violent, who roam on the borders of the lake. At the time of Josephus, says Renan, there were many more trees there, and more careful cultivation, but has not Josephus, that lover of definite features and bright colours, exaggerated the contrast between the dark and sinister shores of the Dead Sea, with its rare bushes, the fruit of which falls away into dust, and the luxurious vegetation of the shores of the Lake of Tiberias? In a climate both wet and hot, the very grain grows as high as bushes, and south of the Dead Sea I have ridden on horseback through maize growing almost higher than my head. The poor Bedouins, camping there under their tents, with no artistic endowments, caring little for luxury, indifferent to the beauties of form, are not for these reasons mere idealists. The dwellers on the river

[1] We must not forget that the smiling Nazareth rejected the Saviour, who had to take refuge on the borders of the Lake.

banks of Tell-Hum are regular thieves, and the taste for brigandage certainly seems the most persistent feature in that part of Galilee which surrounds the burning little basin that the lake becomes during summer. It is true that according to Renan, "The brigandage deeply rooted in Galilee gave much force to these views"[1]—that is to say to that "essentially Galilean" sentiment of indifference in the matter of riches. Jesus was preaching to the converted! In that case they certainly had no resemblance to those who have replaced them in this region!

Certainly we do not suggest that there is nothing new in Galilee, either in the country or its inhabitants. But these changes which are much more profound than the convinced partisans of the unchanging East will believe, require much caution on the part of the critic. Did Renan know these countries, and the mysterious relation between the ancient East and the Islamic and Christian East of the nineteenth century, well enough to have the right to say "in order to grasp this fully one must have been in the East."[2]

Several of his observations are accurate. He acutely noted that there is not in the East too disagreeable a difference between the rich and the poor, above all in the country-side. They all enjoy the same climate, more clement than ours, and the same comforts, for civilization has not there created its artificial requirements. The fruits of the earth, with which the rich are contented, cannot be denied

[1] p. 111. [2] p. 512, French edition.

to the poor. From this arises an equality, if not more from the heart, at any rate more real and more exacting than among ourselves.

Here is a charming example: "In the East the house into which a stranger enters becomes at once a public place. All the village assembles there, the children invade it, and, though dispersed by the servants, always return."[1] It has always been thus, for nature has, at bottom, changed little, and the economic conditions of life in Palestine to-day are more like what they were in the time of Jesus than what they are now in France. It may be seen what a light is cast by the knowledge of these customs on the gospel scenes.

The reader will enjoy another quotation which I do not care to spoil by paraphrasing, and which could not have been written without great insight. "Scholastic education among us draws a profound distinction in respect of personal worth, between those who have received and those who have been deprived of it. It was not so in the East, nor, in general, in the good old times. The state of ignorance in which, among us, owing to our isolated and entirely individual life, those remain who have not passed through the schools, was unknown in those societies where moral culture, and especially the general spirit of the age, was transmitted by the perpetual intercourse of man with man."[2]

The East to-day helps us to understand what was already implied in a literary knowledge of the

[1] p. 120. [2] p. 47.

ancient East. "The Arab, who has never had a teacher, is often, nevertheless, a very superior man; for the tent is a kind of school, always open, where, from the contact of well educated men, there is produced a great intellectual and even literary movement."[1]

This is good, but too flattering: it is, however, a point that should never be forgotten in examining the Johannine question. Was John the son of Zebedee so lacking in culture that he could not have written the fourth gospel because he had not in his youth frequented the Greek schools? Still, it is something that Renan should have made an examination of the conditions in the East to-day and given the benefit of them to Jesus.[2] This is a legitimate line to follow, because it rests on a social state traditional in the East. But it is not in this connection that Renan pronounced with some emphasis "In order to grasp this fully one must have been in the East."[3]

What then is he talking about? The gravest question of all—the miracles. He wishes to explain miracles without too much recourse to the

[1] p. 47.

[2] But he cannot help exaggerating. After having said that Jesus was not what we call ignorant, Renan concludes that in this social state ignorance "is the condition of great things and of great originality." (p. 34). This is too much, for Mohammed himself only stirred up Arabia by means of certain great ideas seized upon by his powerful imagination. Renan's design was clearly to explain, without a shadow of the supernatural, the sublime teaching of Jesus. For the same reason he elevates the Apostles who are simple fishermen; "this calling did not have the extreme humbleness which the rhetoric of preachers would give it, the better to display the miraculous origin of Christianity."

[3] p. 512, French edition.

idea of imposture, yet without altogether excluding it. The Oriental comes in here to give authority to a psychological contradiction. " In the East passion is the soul of everything, and credulity has no bounds. One never sees to the bottom of an Oriental's thoughts, for they often have no bottom for himself. Passion on one side, credulity on the other create imposture."[1]

Doubtless a man may arrive at imposture through impassioned credulity, but it is not the shortest road. Those who know best how to deceive others are not usually the most easily deceived, and so little is the East the explanation of this twisted psychology that Renan the next moment attacks the arguments whereby the Barbarians were converted. Next, to prove that " between the general truth of a principle and the truth of a small fact the man of faith never hesitates ", we are given the history of the holy Ampulla and the coronation of Charles X[2]; elsewhere the miracle of La Salette, with its bibliographical reference,[3] and then Clovis' dove, the virtues of the oriflamme, the supernatural mission of Joan of Arc. Are we still in the East?

To begin with it has to be proved that " fanaticism is always sincere in its thesis and deceitful in its methods of demonstration."[4] Speaking very mildly, we may say that the word " always " is excessive. Voltaire thought differently. His Mahomet was deceitful in his methods of demonstration without being sincere in his thesis. Moreover, one cannot

[1] p. 512, French edition.
[2] p. 513, French edition.
[3] p. xxvii, French edition.
[4] p. 512, French edition.

see that the mixture of fanaticism and deceit is confined to the East. Examples could be quoted from our immediate neighbourhood. But what is most certainly rare everywhere is an overwhelming love of truth, allying itself with easy falsehood. What Renan needed for his thesis was souls at once candid and unscrupulous, open, loyal, disinterested, yet not shrinking from dissimulation in order to succeed. He could not forget "the true character and naïve innocence of the Galilean movement." This innocence had to be allied with deceit described by an euphemism as "self-conscious illusion." To penetrate this enigma he went so far as to break open the secrets of the oriental harem. "Analogies must here be sought in the fleeting sensations of the soul of an oriental woman. Passion, naïveté, renunciation, tenderness, perfidy, idyll, and crime, frivolity and depth, sincerity and falsehood alternate in natures of this sort, and cheat any attempt at a definite estimate."[1] Not a doubt of it! And there are such women in the west also if we are to believe the stories. But what have these morals of melodrama in common with the Idyll and the good folk of Galilee? If Renan owes this *joli type* to his personal observations were they not made at the romantic theatre of the Porte St. Martin? The tricky and sensual being that the Arab storytellers understood a woman to be has not in her these tragic depths.

What the European reader wants to know is whether the Oriental is really more credulous than

[1] p. 516, French edition.

himself. For my own part, I answer unhesitatingly: No—and I am speaking of the European of the twentieth century. I believe that a certain distrust which exists in the depths of his character prevents the Oriental from believing in the absurdities which our credulity so smilingly accepts. However this may be, if he happens to tell a lie to uphold the opinion he has embraced, the Eastern knows that he is lying just as well as we do. It is a pure flourish of style—and not a very brilliant flourish this time—for Renan to find himself unable to penetrate to the bottom of his thought, "for often this bottom has no existence for the man himself." The Eastern being a man, may only be trying to deceive himself by pretending that "necessity has no law," but this maxim did not come to us from Palestine to justify deceit. An Oriental who testifies to a false miracle would be just as conscious of his lie as a nun in one of our convents falsely claiming to have the stigmata. In these matters the East of to-day has nothing to teach us about the East of long ago. Neither the one nor the other are outside the conditions belonging to human nature as such, conditions the same at all times and in all places.

We see to what a slight extent the East was a revelation for Renan. The vision of a Galilean spring created the Galilean idyll. To get rid of miracles he imagined an Eastern figure of Romance. Some of his ideas are accurate, but he neglected the minor details of Archæology, for which he clearly had no taste (as can be seen even in his *Mission de Phénicie*), and which would have bored his readers.

He had not discovered any fifth gospel. He was obliged to return continually to our four gospels, and to use them as documents. But as he considered them of so little worth how could he build up his history?

Art much more than the East was his chief gospel. As a writer, Renan was certainly original, but does this bold intervention of Art, which makes the beauty of the book, make it a book of true history? Has not the desire of making a sentimental effect on a large public damaged the single-minded quest into what the past really was? The Germans, as we have said, bit further into the texts, but they did not dare to treat what was left of them too freely. This was only an artifice, for the materials were cut down beforehand so as to be used according to the plan conceived in their imagination. But they always asked permission of the texts thus to misuse them in a very polite fashion. As Mark was admitted as the oldest and surest witness, his chronology was adhered to as a framework of Christ's life. Renan had to take into account the fourth gospel, in which the succession of events is very different. His scepticism might this time have done him service, and we can imagine a historian of the Life of Jesus following in the order of his facts, sometimes St. John, sometimes one or other of the Synoptics. Since none of them attaches enough importance to the chronological order of the facts to force his own chronology upon us, one might even be tempted to make use of all four.

A historian would have then the absolute right

of reserving judgment in some matters. But he ought not to go beyond a note of interrogation, for what hope has he of establishing a chronology in contradiction with the infrequent agreement of all four gospels? And when there is definite agreement on an important point he should bow before it.

In the name of Art, Renan has dared to break all rules of historical investigation. He had somehow to escape from the uncertainty into which he had been plunged by his unjust depreciation of the evangelists. The only method for a Philosopher imbued with the Hegelian system, was to rediscover the Idea: the thinness of the details matters very little if they express the Idea. "These details are not true to the letter, but they are true with a superior truth, they are more true than the naked truth, in the sense that they are truth rendered expressive and articulate—truth idealized"[1]—and yet he pretends to speak in the name of History. "The historian has one care only, Art and Truth (two inseparable things, for art keeps the secret of the most intimate laws of truth)."[2]

What a fruitful union! Happy is he to whom such a secret has been revealed. Renan has told us what it is—the idea of a living organism which "we have not hesitated to take as our guide in the general arrangement of the narrative."[3] In other words, "in histories such as this the great test that we have got the truth is to have succeeded in combining the texts in such a manner that they shall constitute a logical, probable narrative, harmonious

[1] p. 25. [2] p. ix, French edition. [3] p. 30.

throughout. . . . We should have the general spirit of the work—one of the forms in which it could have existed."[1]

How could this historian fail to see that the last little sentence spoils the whole? Supposing, in fact, that all is in harmony, this gives us a guarantee that things might have happened in this way, that this is one possible combination, but does this make it the only one? Even if we maintain against Boileau that the truth must be likely, it does not follow that everything which seems likely is therefore true.

Will anyone assert that such a complex matter as the arrangement of someone's biography, from texts which have not been edited to make a unity, can be so successful as to exclude all chance of error? It is possible, but to do it we must neither "solliciter les textes,"[2] nor contradict them openly when they are in agreement with one another. And even this liberty Renan allowed himself in the name of the organism which he had conceived.

What was this organism? It was a conception of the development of the preaching of Jesus analogous to that followed by Mohammed. We will not discuss Mohammed, since the chronological order of the *Suras* of the Koran still remains a matter of conjecture, but here is the hypothesis which is made to link the two:

[1] p. 29.

[2] This is translated in the *Everyman* edition as giving the texts an "appreciative interpretation." This does not seem to us to render the full force of Renan's proposed treatment of them: so we give his own words. *Translator's note.*

"There is no great abuse of hypothesis in supposing that a founder of a new religion commences by attaching himself to the moral aphorisms already in circulation in his time, and to the practices which are in vogue; that, when riper, and in full possession of his idea, he delights in a kind of calm and poetical eloquence, remote from all controversy, sweet and free as pure feeling; that he warms by degrees, becomes animated by opposition, and finishes by polemics and strong language."[1]

Of course this idea is put forward with all the doubts, reticences and reserves in which Renan delights, yet it is certainly on these main lines that the *Life of Jesus* is constructed. Without this division it would not exist. The three periods are always distinct, that of the innocent sayings or the Galilean Pastoral, the beautiful moral sermons of the second period, and finally the definite politics of the revolutionary. It may be that examples of such an evolution are to be met with in history, but may we not also conceive that a young revolutionary grew gentle with the passage of time, even to the point of ending with "innocent aphorisms."

Does not history relate many instances of men beginning with an outburst of religious feeling who were able later to hold themselves in with a calm perhaps more divine? Did not St. Francis while always pronouncing innocent sayings, powerfully inaugurate his revolt against those who opposed his voluntary poverty?

[1] p. 30.

But neither conjectures nor comparisons are really of much use here. We must know what the documents say. Renan had a right to place the calling of the disciples before the imprisonment of the Baptist, since that is the order given by the fourth gospel, but he could not, without abdicating his rôle of historian, suppose and recount a whole period of Christ's public ministry before His baptism. The most definite point in the gospel tradition is that the Saviour's baptism inaugurated His mission. And it needed still greater impertinence to write up this imaginary period with matter placed quite late and in very marked circumstances by the evangelists. But Renan clung to a period, the most exquisite of all, before the austere influence of the Baptist. For his portraiture of the change of the charmer into " the revolutionary " and the " sombre giant " he relied—apart from his own exaggeration—upon a change of tone. The familiar conversations in Galilee with His disciples did not in fact require the firmness, we might almost say the vehemence, of Christ's arguments with the Jews. But according to St. Mark (III, 5) the Saviour grew wrathful against the hardness of heart of the Pharisees in Galilee at the beginning. Again, according to the Fourth Gospel, of which Renan here prefers the chronology, the expulsion of the traffickers from the Temple took place at the beginning of The Jerusalem Ministry.[1] The revolutionary had then already begun His work. The " Idea " is a bad counsellor

[1] p. 488 French edition, but this is absolutely contradicted on p. 214 note 1, French edition.

when it claims to govern the texts and extract from them the truth that suits it. Without these transpositions the idyll of Galilee would disappear and be seen as the creation of Renan—his dream of the East. This is what makes the interest of the book for those who do not feel how jarring it is. But criticism has shown as much severity as moral and religious feeling towards this historical forgery. No one has mistaken it for a bit of true metal.

To ennumerate all the violence or "*douces sollicitations*" done to the documents to extract from them the guiding idea of the life of Jesus would be to enter now on the subject of the preaching of the Kingdom of God, to which we shall return later. On this point Renan was obeying a principle which he viewed quite clearly. He was absolutely obliged either to follow the texts or to twist them if they were in contradiction with the Idea.

It is less easy to understand another "artistic" procedure, quite arbitrary and followed out with disconcerting perseverance. The evangelists have thrown into relief certain scenes, or at any rate have told them as special events of which the memory was preserved, on account either of their importance or of the lesson they conveyed. To accept this way of looking at things would have been to acknowledge the historical character of the stories. To this the critic can only half consent. But the artist does not mean to deprive his picture of these picturesque features, and so he generalizes, or, to speak more accurately, he multiplies. He puts in the plural what is really in the singular. St. Matthew is much reproached for having seen two blind men at Jericho where Mark and Luke only knew one; St. Mark for having related two multiplications of loaves. Renan continually turns something which happened only once into a habit, and the way he does this is so strange that his words must be quoted: "A group of men and women, all characterised by the same spirit of childish frankness and simple innocence, adhered to him and said, 'Thou art the Messiah.' As the Messiah was to be the Son of David, they naturally conceded to him this title, synonymous with the former. Jesus allowed it with pleasure to be given to him, although it might cause him some embarrassment, his birth being well known."[1]

No reference is given, and there is good reason for this, for the little scene is quite imaginary. Or, rather, the author has anticipated, multiplied, and placed in Galilee, attributing it to candid and naïve groups, the confession of the blind man of Jericho, and the acclamations of Palm Sunday. In real fact St. Mark greatly insisted, on the contrary, on the Messianic secret, and the care that Jesus took to avoid inopportune worship. After all this, what effect could Peter's confession produce? How can it be said that "He had been the first to recognise Jesus as the Messiah?"[2]

"They said that he used to speak on the mountains with Moses and Elias."[3] This time the texts relating to the transfiguration are quoted, and doubtless this popular "*on dit*," multiplying to any

[1] p. 94. [2] p. 105. [3] p. 170, French edition.

extent such an extraordinary conversation, dispenses Renan from any explanation of the fact.

"He went willingly to Marriage Feasts. One of his miracles was performed, it is said, to enliven a wedding in a small town."[1] This is all he says about the Marriage Feast of Cana. Jesus was so often present at marriages that no doubt he found other means of making them gay!

Here again is a real jewel. "He thus traversed Galilee in the midst of a continual feast. He rode on a mule. In the East this is a good and safe mode of travelling; the large black eyes of the animal, shaded by long eye-lashes, gave it an expression of gentleness. His disciples sometimes surrounded him with a kind of rustic pomp, at the expense of their garments, which they used as carpets."[2]

And in the footnote "Matthew xxi, 7–8." We should need quite a Galilean simplicity not to notice that Renan is amusing himself, that Matthew speaks of a donkey in connection with the public Messianic Coming at the entry into Jerusalem. When the time comes to relate this event the reader will have an indefinite impression of something seen before. . . . He will remember the mule, such a good mode of travelling in the East!

"Women came to pour oil upon his head and perfume on his Feet. His disciples sometimes repulsed them as troublesome."[3] We may distinguish if we will the sinner of Luke vii, from the woman who came to anoint Jesus before His passion, but Renan saw in this action one and the same

[1] p. 119. [2] p. 120. [3] p. 120.

scene transformed by Luke, the friend of sinners, into a scene of pardon. Then why the use of the plural and why in Galilee?

Children "were like a young guard around Jesus, for the inauguration of his innocent royalty, and gave him little ovations which much pleased him, calling him, 'Son of David,' crying Hosannah, and bearing palms around him."[1]

This again is borrowed from the triumph of Bethphage, but wherever in the gospels or elsewhere can be found anything which allows him to write "while joyous Galilee was celebrating in feasts the coming of the Well-Beloved, the sorrowful John, in his prison of Machero, was pining away with expectation and desire."[2]

What a marvellous contrast, perhaps invented to make joyous Galilee richer by a feature borrowed from melancholy Judea! What an artist! but what a critic!

Of Mary, the sister of Martha he writes, "seated at the feet of Jesus she often forgot."[3] Of Jesus, "He often quoted the passage in Isaiah. . ."[4] "He often sat on the mount of Olives. . . . He cried out in his moments of bitterness, 'Oh, Jerusalem' . . ."[5]

We have already pointed out that according to Renan the Washing of the Feet did not take place before the Last Supper, but to make up for this it often happened in other circumstances, and the Eucharist was a rite practised by Jesus as

[1] p. 121. [2] p. 97. [3] p. 189. [4] p. 136. [5] p. 190.

often as you like, excepting only on the eve of His Death.

Renan says something else, not only arbitrary, in two ways, but which seems, moreover, to cast a shade on the Purity of Our Lord. "He protected those who wished to honour him. Thus children and women adored him. The reproach of alienating from their families these gentle creatures, always easily misled [*séduites*] was one of the most frequent charges of his enemies."[1]

These lines are prominent in the *Vie Populaire* (p. 116) naturally without any reference. What can the reader, simple or otherwise, think except that this reproach occurs frequently in the gospels? The complete edition sends us in a note to one solitary text (Luke xxiii, 2), in which the Jews denounce Our Lord to Pilate—and even this complaint is an addition of Marcion's which no critical editor has dared to introduce into the authentic text. According to the Latin Variant the reproach even here (Luke xxiii, 5) has a religious character—that Jesus was turning the women and children away from baptisms and purifications.

In Renan's context something else might be supposed, and one is led to suspect that if the reproach was so frequent it had some foundation—at any rate, in appearance

When the evangelists give us sayings of Our Lord, the same fundamentally but different superficially, scrupulous commentators, rather than admit a slight variance in the tradition, say: these are two different

[1] p. 121.

discourses. The critics have criticised this unsparingly. What do they think of the sovereign caprice with which Renan plays with the texts. Is this history or a historical novel. And if it is a novel, has he even succeeded in drawing a probable picture of his hero?

IV

The Mission and the Person of Jesus.

We must finally approach the most decisive question of all—that of the office and the preaching of Jesus, His character, and His Person.

Renan perfectly understood the illusion of the liberal exegesis dominant at that time (about 1863) in the German Theological Universities. But, perhaps he did not fully understand it until after publishing the *Life of Jesus*, for it is in the definitive preface to his thirteenth edition that he expressly makes a break with this method.

It was to set oneself too easy a task to write the Life of Christ, slurring over the miracles, watering down the Master's assertions, about His Mission as the Messiah, about His rulership over the coming Kingdom of God, His certitude of the supernatural character of this Kingdom and of its imminence. They would sketch the features of a remarkable personality, powerful in his outlook, without too much mystery in his teaching; this figure was placed in the framework of a coherent and probable history: the whole destined for the edification of those dwelling in the heart of modern German Protestantism. The French critic protested against all this in the name of History. He called it the work of Theology, but it was rather the attempt of naturalism to substitute itself noiselessly and gradually for faith in Revelation. He blamed these theologians for still remaining slaves to dogma, like a bird whose wings have only been slightly clipped, yet gradually putting forward very sceptical views because they were offering them to a public which shrank from the marvellous.

He himself, both as critic and as historian, chose to be as free as air. People may say what they like. He does not hesitate to attribute to Jesus miracles—or rather the intention to perform them, messianic claims and illusory apocalyptic theories about the Kingdom of God.

But as we have said, if this bird kept his liberty and all his feathers he still had a string tied to his foot, because Christ *must* remain the Founder of a pure Religion. Renan then confronted more difficulties than the Germans, but did not get rid either of hesitations or contradictions. It must be agreed that such a subject admits of hesitations and demands delicate shading, but contradictions are no solution in the eyes of reasonable people, whether they be the author's own contradictions, more or less wrapped up in confused statements, or those which he has been driven to locating in his hero's mind. In one supreme contradiction all these minor ones are summed up. The Jesus of liberal Protestants could be admired because He made no supernatural claims. The Jesus of Catholics is to be adored because He is truly what He claimed to be, the Son of God, one with the Father. The Jesus of Renan, whom he wanted to admire and whom he offers for our admiration, inspires in reality nothing but contempt or pity. Scarcely can his advocate succeed in pleading extenuating circumstances arising from a peculiar state of mind due to the period and the country in which he lived.

Let us look first at the mission Jesus declared to be His and the rôle that He claimed to play.

At moments Renan reduces the person of Christ even more than does the liberal school, " One would make Jesus out a wise man, another a philosopher, a patriot, others again a man of good works, a moralist or a saint. He was none of these things. He was a charmer "[1] At that rate he would have remained faithful to the idyllic preaching of the Kingdom of God. And in fact that was all which we are to believe was left of His work. " The essential work of Jesus was to create around him a circle of disciples, whom he inspired with boundless affection, and in whom he laid the germ of his doctrine."[2] A germ is not much, and this particular germ contained no doctrine: "Jesus has founded the absolute religion, excluding nothing and determining nothing unless it be the spirit [*le sentiment*]."[3]

Here we see the Jesus of this more than liberal theologian, the Jesus that Renan would really have preferred, but he had to take account of the Jesus of history, called by the Catholic Church Jesus

[1] p. xxiii, French edition. [2] p. 235.
[3] p. 237.

Christ, and Who must, therefore, have said something on the question of the Messiah.

According to the synoptics Christ for a long time kept His Messianic title secret, but He consented to be treated as Messiah at the triumph of Bethphage, and He confessed Himself to be both Messiah and Son of God before the Sanhedrin. According to Renan He took pleasure in being called the Messiah in Galilee, but He did not choose to speak before His judges. "If we may believe one version, the high-priest then adjured him to say if he were the Messiah; Jesus confessed it, and proclaimed before the assembly the near approach of his heavenly reign."[1] It is not *one* but three versions that we are to believe.[2] Renan, however, objects "The fourth gospel knows nothing of such a scene."[3] Inclining in the direction of not believing the story he even excuses Our Saviour "The courage of Jesus, who had resolved to die, renders this narrative superfluous. It is probable that here, as when before Hanan, he remained silent."[4]

But then, why was He condemned? His judges were only seeking pretexts. So be it, but still they had to allege them.

But anyhow Jesus did call Himself the Messiah. What did He mean by that?

By the year 1863 John Weiss had not yet inaugurated the idea of a more or less coherent escha-

[1] p. 214.

[2] Matthew xxvi, 64; Mark xiv, 62; Luke xxii, 69.

[3] French Edition, footnote to p. 409.

[4] p. 214.

tological Messiahship, but the critics were already preoccupied with the question of what Jesus meant by the Kingdom of God, and it was fully realized that He associated Himself with the end of all things. They were already asking whether Jesus intended to found a Moral and Spiritual Kingdom of God, or whether He was expecting the imminent arrival of a Supernatural Kingdom of God.

These two ideas could and should be united. According to the Catholic explanation there is no contradiction, since the moral and spiritual Kingdom of God was actually about to be inaugurated by the Divine intervention shown in Christ's resurrection and in the Mission of the Holy Ghost. There is, however, one difficulty. This is to distinguish in the Words of Jesus what is to be understood of the Reign of God upon earth, and of the Kingdom of God in Heaven, what marks the foundation of His Kingdom, coinciding with the rejection of the Jewish people and the fall of Jerusalem, and what refers to the consummation of all things and the end of the world. This we say is a difficulty, perhaps because the perspectives of the two events seem confused, perhaps because the same symbolic expressions are used in both cases. This chiaroscuro is in the very nature of things, for Jesus was the last of the prophets, and in a certain sense continued their preaching. For them the Messianic Advent was not merely seen afar off, but it marked the end of time; their revelations went no farther. Christ unquestionably distinguished the times but He did not alter His terminology. The pious impatience of believers did the rest. They could not at first conceive that the Founder of the Kingdom of God upon earth should not be its Ruler on earth; they had to get accustomed to the rule of the Holy Ghost instead and the spiritual presence of Christ.

It is impossible to admit that Jesus had in mind a spiritual kingship, a regeneration working for men and through men, that He was the most enlightened and powerful of religious reformers, foreseeing and dominating the future; and that He preached at the same time an intervention of God destructive of nature itself, and thus sweeping away the very garden in which the new morality had to grow.

This, however, was the wager that Renan undertook to win.

He proposes two solutions, no doubt to give us a choice since they are contradictory. The earlier and more timid manner of criticism suggested that one conception succeeded the other in the Master's mind. Renan imagines three conceptions, but the first—that offered for the benefit of the gentle and innocent Galileans—can easily be joined with the idea of a spiritual Kingdom. This was the real idea of Jesus; the other was only a late and transitory error. The passage is categorical and must be quoted in its entirety.

"In the later periods of his life Jesus believed that this reign would be realised in a material form by a sudden renovation of the world. But doubtless this was not his first idea. The admirable moral which he draws from the thought of God as Father is not that of enthusiasts who believe the world is near its end, and who prepare themselves by asceticism for a chimerical catastrophe; it is that of men who have lived and still would live. 'The Kingdom of God is within you,' said he to those who sought with subtilty for external signs. The realistic conception of the divine advent was but a cloud, a transient error, which his death has made us forget."[1]

But we have not to wait long for Renan to contradict himself. "A radical revolution, embracing even nature itself, was the fundamental idea of Jesus."[2] Doubtless it was also the first thought which he announced openly after his baptism, that is to say when his teaching became public and systematic. The 'Kingdom of God' was approaching, and it was he, Jesus, who was that 'Son of Man' whom Daniel had beheld in his vision as the divine herald of the last and supreme revelation. . . . "The application which Jesus made of it to himself was, therefore, the proclamation of his messiah-ship, and the affirmation of the coming catastrophe in which he was to figure as Judge."[3]

It was possible, however, to contradict oneself still more completely. The democratic Kingdom of God did not greatly preoccupy Christ's mind. There remains the Kingdom of God a literal fulfilment of "the apocalyptic visions concerning the Messiah," and the spiritual kingdom. "As to these two conceptions of the Kingdom of God, Jesus appears

[1] p. 71. [2] p. 87. [3] pp. 93-4.

always to have held them simultaneously."[1] In contradicting himself Renan introduces a contradiction into Our Saviour's mind. Moreover, he is triumphant concerning it:

"The two parts of his system, or, rather, his two conceptions of the Kingdom of God, rest one on the other, and this mutual support has been the cause of his incomparable success."[2] These words would be fully justified if, as in the Catholic tradition, these two conceptions were complementary. But we must ask here, as Renan did just now, whether the moral outlook of Jesus was that of a visionary who believes the world to be near its end?

This idea certainly does not persist in Renan's mind. On the contrary "it is because his thought was two-sided that it has been fruitful. His chimera has not had the fate of so many others which have crossed the human mind, because it concealed a germ of life which, having been introduced, thanks to the covering of fable, into the bosom of humanity, has thus brought forth eternal fruits."[3]

What an elegant phrase! But the critic knows that it will not work. He is frightened, and this is almost comic, of being taken for an apologist. He has only been fair, "And let us not say," he continues, "that this is a benevolent interpretation, imagined in order to clear the honour of our great Master from the cruel contradiction inflicted on his dreams by reality."[4]

[1] pp. 106–7.
[2] p. 157.
[3] p. 160.
[4] p. 160–1.

What a good apostle is this last apostle of the great Master's! The peroration becomes a cry for pity:

"Let us pardon him his hope of a vain apocalypse, and of a second coming in great triumph upon the clouds of heaven." For after all, Jesus was not so very positive. "Perhaps these were the errors of others rather than his own."[1] It may, in fact, all be summed up as not having happened, but what more did liberal exegesis demand?

In the same way in which Christ's doctrine looked two ways, so his acts were directed to two ends. "He proposed to himself to create a new state of humanity and *not merely* to prepare the end of that which was in existence."[2]

This "not merely" would be entertaining if it were not contemptible, not only on the subject of Jesus and the Gospel, but in any kind of historical work. All these pretty sayings fade away before the words that follow: "This morality attributed to the latter days, is found to be the eternal morality, that which has saved humanity."[3] But do these words ring true?

For this swinging back and forth continues to soothe us—or to send us to sleep?—for page after page; antistrophe follows strophe in the song, pictures float before our eyes, their colours mingling in the soft light. . . . Now we know exactly what the "Kingdom of God" is! "The favourite phrase of Jesus continues, therefore, full of an eternal beauty.

[1] p. 161. [2] p. 161. [3] p. 161.

A kind of exalted divination seems to have maintained it in a vague sublimity, embracing at the same time various orders of truth."[1] A man may well be proud of having grasped this!

Can the thunder of the gospel preaching still awaken those who have taken all this morphine?

Those who have still some confidence in common sense will pause at these lucid lines: "That there may have been a contradiction between the belief in the approaching end of the world and the general moral system of Jesus, conceived in prospect of a permanent state of humanity, nearly analogous to that which now exists, no one will attempt to deny."[2]

The problem put forward by independent criticism has not then been solved. For nothing is done by involving the fortune of Christianity in a contradiction: "The world seeks both to change and to last."[3] No doubt—and that is what Our Lord proposed. But He cannot have seriously proposed to change a world that was not going to last! The prison chaplain does not suggest to the condemned criminal a change of life, but a preparation for death. These compositions are fair game for the eschatologists.

Exposed as we are to the flow of their very cutting affirmations we are not sorry to point out in return that Renan's imagination had some limits, and to recall his eulogy of the eternal morality of Jesus, the true founder of the Church! "That Jesus was never entirely absorbed in his apocalyptic ideas is proved, moreover, by the fact that at the

[1] p. 164. [2] p. 91. [3] p. 91.

very time he was most preoccupied with them he laid with rare forethought the foundation of a Church destined to endure."[1]

Yet things even reach the point where we have to be grateful to him for not turning Our Lord into a revolutionary Messiah. He found it amusing to give us a momentary fright: " A movement which had much more influence upon Jesus was that of Judas the Gaulonite, or Galilean."[2] But everything is explained "Jesus more wise and far removed from all sedition, profited by the fault of his predecessor, and dreamed of another Kingdom and another deliverance."[3] *Lucus a non lucendo* then.

And, by the way, we must understand after the same fashion this pleasant paradox: " Notwithstanding all their enormous defects—hard, egotistical, scoffing, cruel, narrow, subtle and sophistical—the Jewish people are the authors of the finest movement of disinterested enthusiasm which history records."[4] This means through Jesus, yet " far from Jesus having continued Judaism, he represents the rupture with the Jewish spirit."[5]

These are real fooleries in criticism and would elsewhere be judged severely. But as people listen to them let us take advantage of an assertion, strongly upheld in the course of this book, against those who only see in Jesus the last prophet of Israel and the prophet of apocalyptic Judaism. These believers in a consistent eschatology are convinced that everyone at that time was in agreement as to the idea of the

[1] p. 165. [2] p. 61. [3] p. 62.
[4] p. 56. [5] p. 242.

Kingdom of God. Renan answered them beforehand: " This reign of God upon earth naturally led to the most diverse interpretations. To Jewish theology the " Kingdom of God " is most frequently only Judaism itself—the true religion, the monotheistic worship, piety." [1]

In His preaching of the Kingdom of God Jesus was then no mere echo. He was announcing a new work; in the unity of His own thought He was bringing together and uniting the ancient foreshadowing. He dominated His own and future ages. What then was He?

A wise man, said the liberal school, a religious mind, the very genius of religion; an inspired prophet say to-day the eschatologists; not even a saint according to Renan, a charmer, who became a religious revolutionary, a sombre giant and alas! a worker of miracles, a thing which must imply dissimulation.

We now reach the most repugnant part of the task of a Catholic critic. Let us get it over quickly.[2]

[1] p. 70.

[2] For this reason we confine ourselves to pointing out only in a note Renan's strange position on the question of the " brethren " of our Lord. His real brothers are not those whose names are usually given, for he admits, with St. Jerome, that James, Joseph, Simon and Jude, mentioned by Mark (vi, 3) and by Matthew (xiii, 55) are cousins german, sons of Mary, sister of the Mother of Jesus, and Cleophas. He even suggests that the expression " brethren of the Lord " evidently constituted in the primitive Church, a kind of " order " parallel to the Apostolate (Note to p. 26, French edition). It would not be possible to give stronger proof that the word " brethren " must not be taken literally—but all the same Renan did give Jesus brothers and sisters. Only " their names are so little known that when the evangelist put in the mouth of the men of Nazareth the enumeration of the brothers according to natural relationship, the names of the sons of Cleophas first presented themselves to him." p. 44.

The charmer only existed for one period. He was the hero of the Pastoral of Galilee: "His amiable character accompanied doubtless by one of those lovely faces which sometimes appear in the Jewish race, threw around him a fascination which no one . . . could escape."[1] It was "by his pure and sweet beauty" that Jesus "calmed the troubled nature"[2] of Mary Magdalen. Renan knows, too, that He was "no doubt more beloved than loving."[3] "These good Galileans had never heard discourses so adapted to their cheerful imaginations. They admired him, they encouraged him"[4] The Kingdom of God was coming, the word paradise summed up the dreams of all: "a delightful garden, where the charming life which was led here below would be continued for ever."[5] "Charm" is often repeated and also "gaiety." The disciples who surround Our Lord are a "joyous and wandering"[6] band, "His gentle gaiety found expression in lively ideas and amiable pleasantries."[7]

This charming carpenter, these "beautiful creatures" who flock around him and adore him, these simple Galileans, are purely an artistic creation. M. Schweitzer compares them to the statues of saints sold in the Place Saint-Sulpice. This comparison is irritating from the mouth of a German, for several of these types offered for our devotion come from Germany. But, anyhow, we get the same

[1] p. 71. [2] p. 102. [3] p. 67. [4] p. 96. [5] pp. 121–2. [6] p. 109. [7] p. 120.

impression of insipidity. This perfume comes from the East, like pastilles of the harem. The science of history loses its dignity by begging for public favour with sentimental ditties. The historian, conscious of his obligations, evokes the ardent figure of Jesus going from town to town and preaching, for for that had He come. He preached indeed the Kingdom of God: "The Kingdom of God is at hand. Do penance."[1]

These were His first words after the baptism according to the synoptics. Renan, who has created out of his own head a previous period of teaching, attributes this to the influence of John who preached penance.[2]

But it is impossible to see in what this influence consisted, and it was "by the natural progress of his own thought" that the "delightful moralist" became the "transcendent revolutionary."[3] The thing that precipitated this natural progress was the first visit to Jerusalem, the severe aspect of which is thrown into strong relief against the clear vision of the lake. The opposition between a cult bristling with observances, and directed by priests, and the pure religion of the Father could not be more marked. Jesus was then shocked by all He saw in the Temple:

[1] Mark i, 14.

[2] Here is his solitary reason, "But if it is true (as the Synoptics tell us) that John recognised Jesus at once and gave him a great welcome it is to be supposed that Jesus was already a master of some renown" (note to p. 109, French edition). This supposition is in contradiction with the four gospels, and would it in any case authorise Renan to create a period by making use of texts relating to another later period?

[3] p. 86

He "returned to Galilee, having completely lost his Jewish faith and filled with revolutionary ardour."

But was this the first journey to Jerusalem, and how came it that the Master's impressions there were so new and so strong? We must not ask the author to find textual support for his views. The synoptics place the parable of the old garments and old bottles near the beginning of Christ's ministry in Galilee; St. John places the expulsion of the traffickers from the Temple at the beginning of the first entry into Jerusalem. The chapter "First Attempts on Jerusalem" has, therefore, only the value of a symbol, and we do not seek to deny that the abrogation of the Jewish law was logically part of Christ's mission; we only assert that He did not understand it after the fashion or at the time that His historian imagines.

A still more serious thing is that the conversion of the delightful moralist into the revolutionary obliged him to become a healer. This, too, is in absolute contradiction with the historical sources. The miracles began in fact in Galilee, and were numerous from the very beginning of His public ministry there. We shall return later to the explanations give by Renan, one of which drove him into attacking Our Saviour's sincerity. He dared to blacken Him by an accusation of dissimulation, at the same time that he defended—or rather excused—Him.

The rights of criticism have been defended. If, people say, pious souls are hurt by the large edition of the *Life of Jesus* so much the worse for them. Renan did not write for them; he had a perfect right to put before an enlightened public the results of his researches. But he did not stop at this. "I have thought I ought to distil from the Life of Jesus a small volume in which nothing should be a drawback to pious souls who do not care about higher criticism."[1]

He does not think it necessary to warn these pious souls that their Christian faith will be injured or even lost in reading it. What did he want to do? Doubtless to spare the feelings of those who look upon Christ as a saint? He offers them "A Christ of white marble . . . cut out of one block, a Christ as pure and simple as the feeling that created him."[2] And he adds "Mon Dieu, perhaps this is the truest presentment. Who knows if there are not moments when everything human is immaculate? These moments do not last long, but they exist."[3] And doubtless these moments did not last long in the life of Jesus. He *had* to succeed. "To conceive good, in fact, is not enough; it must be made to succeed among men. For this less pure methods are needed."[4] In short Christ had to make up his mind to work miracles.

Is the insinuation less evil because it is wrapped up in equivocal and confused formularies. What it means is: Jesus had recourse to dissimulation, and

[1] Footnote to Preface.
[2] *Edition populaire.*
[3] *Edition populaire*, p. vi.
[4] *Edition populaire*, p. iv.

Christianity is the result of his lies.[1] O, Renan did not say it in these words!

Let us return to the *Life of Jesus* itself, which was written "without a shade of *arrière pensée*."[2]

Here is the general excuse which the author finds for his great master. "Troubled minds cannot have the clearness of good sense. But it is only troubled minds that are powerful in their action. . . . The state of the documents does not enable us to say in which cases the illusion was self-conscious. All that can be said is that sometimes it was so. The life of a healer cannot be lived for years without a man being driven into a corner time after time, without his hand being forced by the public. . . . He begins in simplicity, credulity, absolute innocence: he ends by all sorts of embarrassments and, to uphold the divine power which is failing he escapes from these embarrassments by desperate expedients. . . . Did not Joan of Arc more than once make her voices speak according to the need of the moment? If the story of the secret revelation made by her to Charles VII has some foundation, which it is hard to deny, this innocent girl must have presented as the effect of supernatural intuition what she had learnt by a confidence."[3]

[1] Again he wrote "When we have effected by our scruples what they accomplished by their falsehoods, we shall have the right to be severe upon them. . . . The only culprit in such cases is humanity, willing to be deceived." (p. 148). The only reticence in this passage omitted in the *Vie Populaire* is that the name of our Lord is not spoken, but it is impossible not to see that His courage in falsehood is being placed in opposition with Renan's timid honesty!

[2] *Edition populaire*, p. iv.

[3] p. xxv, French edition.

As we cannot always be losing our temper we will only notice here the historian's absent-mindedness. So little was the secret revelation of Joan a desperate expedient, that it came at the beginning of her mission. It was by it that she acquired her authority. In the same way the miracles of Christ drew his disciples after Him. More than one nun, mad with vanity, has sought to escape from embarrassment by a false pretence of revelations. The Inquisition—especially in Spain—had the bad taste not to declare them innocent. It is all very well for Renan to add the case of Bab. He was a sort of Freemason, erected by the crowd into prophet and healer, and would, for very little, have been persuaded by the legend about himself into working miracles "if the Persian Government had not removed him from the influence of his disciples." "This man," says Renan without a smile, "told me that having almost been a prophet he knew how these things happened, and that they took place exactly as described in my *Life of Jesus*."[1] Jesus, too, would almost have preferred to make no dupes. "We may, therefore, conclude that his reputation of thaumaturgist was imposed upon him, that he did not resist it much, but also that he did nothing to aid it, and that at all events, he felt the vanity of popular opinion on this point."[2] The culprits being so numerous, their accomplices may be absolved. But all the same this superior disdain of public opinion is very self-conscious. This explanation does not satisfy you? Then suppose Jesus to be in good faith: He acted,

[1] Footnote to French edition, p. 274. [2] pp. 153–4.

not to win success, but from simple good nature: "Convinced that the touching of his robe, the imposition of his hands, the application of his saliva, did good to the sick, he would have been unfeeling had he refused to those who suffered a solace in his power to bestow."[1] But then, in what way was Jesus culpable of conscious deceit since He was Himself completely deceived? "One of his most deeply-rooted opinions was that by faith and prayer man has entire power over nature."[2] Then with what is He to be reproached?

It would have been a shame to rob pious souls of these edifying things, so they find a place in the popular edition. In the longer book the educated are told that these questions really are not asked in the East. "To the deeply earnest races of the West conviction means sincerity to one's self. But sincerity to one's self has not much meaning to Oriental peoples little accustomed to the subtleties of a critical spirit."[3]

Was Jesus, the Eastern, more honest in the testimony He gave of Himself? For Jesus declared Himself the Son of God. Doubtless, assents liberal criticism, He certainly was the Father's best son, He was conscious of being the one most tenderly united with Him. This is simple, but it is really too simple for this tragic story. The Messianists are not startled either: they believe that they know the Son of God to have been merely the synonym of Messiah; Christ was deluded, like so many others. Renan better understood the demands of the texts. The

[1] p. 152. [2] p. 150. [3] p. 147.

two errors to avoid were to reduce so august an expression to a banal affirmation or to take it literally—which for the unbelieving critic would imply a pride verging on madness, or a definite imposture. Failing one good solution, Renan offers us the choice among several. Here is a very reasonable Jesus. "He believes himself more than an ordinary man, but separated from God by infinite distance. He is Son of God; but all men are, or may become so, in diverse degrees."[1] A liberal theologian could not have put it better. A historian must take note of something else." Jesus did not preach his opinions, he preached himself."[2] This would be excessive in an ordinary man. "It is regarded as vain glory by those who see in the new teaching only the personal fantasy of the founder; but it is the finger of God to those who see the result. The fool stands side by side here with the inspired man; only the fool never succeeds. It has not yet been given to insanity to influence seriously the progress of humanity."[3] This is a very good general reflection, but it was thought offensive to pious ears, and cut out of the popular edition—doubtless because of this pride so little excused by its results.

We must also congratulate Renan for having avoided the fantastic exegesis of the liberals, who place at the baptism the moment when Jesus became conscious of His title of Son of God. "The first thought of Jesus, a thought so deeply rooted in him that it had probably no beginning, and formed part of his very being, was that he was the Son of

[1] p. 144. [2] p. 69. [3] pp. 69–70.

God, the friend of his Father, the doer of his will."[1]

Jesus, in fact, had a high estimate of himself. "Even the title of prophet or messenger of God responded no longer to his ideas. The position which he attributed to himself was that of a superhuman being."[2] Our Lord's claims then have grown as time went on?

How is such pride to be excused—except by its results—if Christ's claim is not legitimate? Here the East cannot help us for the Jew was *par excellence* the adorer of One God. But Jesus had "a high conception of the divinity—which he did not owe to Judaism."[3]

He was neither deist nor pantheist. In fact, is it quite certain that Jesus was not a Hegelian before Hegel? "In his poetic conception of nature one breath alone penetrates the universe: the breath of man is that of God. . . . The transcendent idealism of Jesus never permitted him a very clear notion of his own personality. He is his Father; his Father is he. He lives in his disciples; he is everywhere with them; his disciples are one, as he and his Father are one. The idea to him is all."[4] This is the same explanation as that given of the miracles. Is it surprising that Jesus worked miracles as all men had the power to work them? He was the Son of God, but that really meant nothing since one breath alone penetrates the universe. After this it seems rather futile to return to the

[1] p. 87. [2] p. 124. [3] p. 68. [4] p. 144.

accusation of fraud. "The need Jesus had of obtaining credence, and the enthusiasm of his disciples, heaped up contradictory notions."[1]

This is the re-appearance of Reimarus or Voltaire. Renan held one of their cards which he did not want to part with. This time he spoke clearly: "I have wished my book to retain its value even at the day when people will come to regard a certain degree of fraud as an element inseparable from religious history. . . . As a reaction from the brutal explanations of the eighteenth century we must not fall into hypotheses which would imply effects without a cause."[2]

German criticism hesitated before the dictum "all the contributors to a legend are either deceived or deceivers." It retained respect for Christ's sincerity. But who knows? There may be a return to Voltaire, and Renan knew perfectly well that he was tending in that direction. He only wanted to avoid being brutal, but one may be quite brutal in velvet gloves; the finest and most graceful irony when it tries to be unctuous, underlines perfidy rather than conceals it. Renan never treated history more cavalierly than by this fancy picture of a Jesus neither deist nor pantheist—but perhaps rather more pantheist—unless by attributing to Our Saviour this need "of obtaining credence."

He aimed, however, at presenting the reader with the true historical Jesus as he understood Him, purely man but a great man of incomparable moral and religious grandeur. Has he succeeded in draw-

[1] p. 147. [2] pp. xxv and xxvii, French edition.

ing a character—I will not say faultless—for he slipped in the faults most sympathetically when saying all he really thought, even in his "Christ of white marble"—but has he drawn the character of a man in harmony with Himself and with the work He accomplished? Is this Jesus probable? Is it probable that He should have been the founder of pure religion as Renan chose to think.

The most different features are not always incompatible. A man might be a charmer and at the shock of contradiction become "harsh and capricious," an exquisite personality may have fits of ill humour[1] and wrath[2]. Nor would it be surprising for a young democrat to be ambitious and to make concessions to public opinion.

But there is something which does not hang together: this candour and purity, this moral grandeur, this aspiration towards the holiness of the Father cannot be reconciled with dissimulation, and with a word which Renan rejects only after suggesting it—jugglery. "It is especially impossible," he says, "to ascertain whether the offensive circumstances attending [the miracles], the groanings, the strugglings, and other features savouring of jugglery, are really historical."[3]

It is incomprehensible that a son of God, believing Himself enlightened from on high, offering Himself

[1] p. 178.

[2] Renan (who would have believed it?) is transported with admiration at our Lord's invectives against the Pharisees, "Incomparable traits, worthy of a Son of God! A God alone knows how to kill after this fashion."

[3] p. 151.

to die for His work, knowing that His death will be man's salvation, that this Messiah with His voluntary immolation[1] should have practised little tricks to give Himself importance in men's eyes and should have made up His mind in order to succeed to use artifices which He despised. And a man who usurped a superhuman title, who believed himself to be one with God, at a time when neither Hegel nor Nietzche existed, and when every pious Jew bent the knee before one true God was not far removed from madness.[2]

Madness has ever been powerless: cheating not always. But in the moral order it has never achieved anything but dishonour and the ruin of souls. If indeed such be the portrait of Jesus: if his burning words, his zeal in God's service, so clear and so pure, sometimes veiled unstraightforward ideas, if the goodness which overflowed in miracles, was subordinated to the thought of success, if his *morale* was in danger of failing, when his falsehood was discovered, can Renan still call such a man his great master?

Simple common sense could not be satisfied by this sort of "playing round" of a super man; psychology protests against such a combination of things incompatible; history has never seen similar phenomena;

[1] "As to Jesus He became confirmed in the idea that He was about to die, but that His death would save the world", p. 203.

[2] "We will admit then, without hesitation, that acts which would now be considered acts of illusion or folly held a large place in the life of Jesus" (p. 154). And Christian abnegation "was originated, not by the refined and cheerful moralist of earlier days, but by the sombre giant whom a kind of grand presentiment was withdrawing, more and more, out of the pale of humanity," p. 175.

criticism easily perceives the falsity of such a construction.

Renan made use of the fourth gospel, not only for its historical facts, but also to penetrate into the intercourse of Jesus with His Father. He uses the last discourses especially John xvii, "which well express one side of the psychology of Jesus although they cannot be thought of as true historical documents."[1] How can such a remark be taken seriously? He was then employing St. John to describe Our Lord's psychological state. But then he had to expect to hear Him assert His unity with the Father, that is to say His divinity. Those critics who, resolved to reduce Jesus to human proportions, resolutely shut the door against St. John, obeyed a surer instinct. Renan thought he could bring off even this paradox by means of *nuances*, attenuations, prodigies of balancing. He has been the only man to attempt such a stroke. Criticism has judged it a failure and has considered that in order to water down Our Lord's affirmations even many of the features of the synoptic gospels must be cut out. But has anyone the right thus to simplify his task? And can a man be sufficient for a divine task? I would only ask those who do not believe, but who think with Renan that an attempt should be made to solve *the question really raised by the documents*[2] to try what they would call the hypothesis of the divinity of Christ. Instantly the difficulties disappear: for God had the right to demand a supreme degree of

[1] p. 254, French edition, note 4.

[2] Italics ours. Translator.

love, God did not deceive men by using His power to serve His goodness, God the Son usurped nothing in declaring Himself equal to the Father. Then with a less hostile outlook they will approach the study of the miracles which proved to His disciples the mission of the Son of God.

V

The Miracles

We need not again go into the question of what, according to Renan, Christ did about miracles. Naturally he never worked any, but he certainly consented to do things that might pass as such. Anyhow it amounted to very little, and he only began late and unwillingly. His culpability is lessened by the necessity of succeeding and even by his ignorance of the laws of nature. He was only an accessory.

But anyhow, in common parlance there are miracles in the gospel, they cannot really be eliminated, they were not all invented later. Renan is determined to admit that miracles have been related by eyewitnesses.[1] Strauss had not grasped all the data of the problem: his denial of the miracles was the pious opinion of a theology anxious to clear Our Lord of the accusation. It remained to be shown how eye-witnesses could have related non-existent miracles. Renan did not lessen this difficulty; according to his favourite method he called upon all the different solutions furnished up to date by German criticism.

[1] "Let us absolutely remove a very widely held idea that miracles are not reported by an eye-witness," p. 505, French edition.

To begin with he clears the ground by cutting out a good number of miracles, for his hypothesis did not compel him to put them all to the account of eye-witnesses. Strauss was generally wrong in seeing in them only a combination of memories and texts all worked up by the creative energy of the community. But this explanation might come in usefully. The preface to the thirteenth edition teaches us that "out of a hundred supernatural stories eighty are entirely the creation of the popular imagination."[1] It is a large proportion; moreover the author has carefully abstained from going over the detailed argumentation of Strauss, the artificial character of which was only too evident.[2]

When the miracle is a really first class one, like the resurrection of Lazarus, the reality must somehow be reduced to nothing, the confusion must be as complete as possible. Renan insists strongly on the importance of the fact, and the place it holds in Our Lord's life before His Passion: one would think he was about to declare it historical.[3] To solve the riddle Strauss and Reimarus together are not more than sufficient. There has been a muddle between the Lazarus of the parable, of the rich man, and Simon the Leper the brother of Martha and Mary. The two sisters suggested to Our Lord to engineer

[1] p. xxi, French edition.

[2] "The criticism of the details of the Gospel texts especially has been done by M. Strauss in a manner which leaves little to be desired" (p. 3). His book is "well planned, accurate, witty and conscientious, although spoiled in general by too close an adherence to one hypothesis" (Note to p. xxxviii, French edition.)

[3] pp. 197–8.

a resurrection as the marvel most likely to strike the incredulous people of Jerusalem. Christ refused. "He may have added 'Lazarus might return, and they would not believe.' Later, strange misconceptions arose. The hypothesis became a fact."[1] The arguments of the German critic, difficult to follow, are brightened by comparisons: do Martha and Mary seem to you rather unscrupulous? "Imagine a legitimist lady reduced to helping Heaven to save Joas. Would she hesitate?"[2] Was he afraid of a resurrection of Charles X?

We still have twenty per cent. of the miracles to explain. "Out of the mass of supernatural events narrated in the gospels and Acts, I have tried in five or six cases to show how the illusion might have arisen."[3] Paulus had been more courageous: his example having served as a lesson Renan was very anxious not to incur the ridicule he had aroused—chiefly by the error of posing as a theologian. A non-theological critic can and ought, he held, to put forward this sort of hypothesis.[4] Why did he not do so more frequently? Their effectiveness may be judged. I have not found the number of five or six from the Gospels and the Acts—but here is the story of the multiplication of the loaves. We are "in the desert"—and Renan, who has seen the places ought to know that on the shores of the lake one is not, speaking accurately, in the desert.[5] However that may be, "By exercising an extreme

[1] p. 197.
[2] p. 516, French edition.
[3] p. xxi, French edition.
[4] p. xxi, note 1, French edition.
[5] Matthew xiv, 13, speaks of "a desert place."

frugality, the holy band was enabled to live there, and in this there was naturally seen a miracle."[1] Was it so natural to turn so natural a fact into a miracle? The worthy Paulus did at least bring in camels loaded with provisions!

The author of so many subtle books was too witty to run such a risk often. He had, however, to give us a general theory. Out of the sixteen pages (reduced to three in the *Vie Populaire*)—of the chapter on miracles the greater number are charitably devoted to clearing Our Lord's character. There is very little space left to go into the question of fact. To sum up, "Almost all the miracles which Jesus thought he performed appear to have been miracles of healing."[2] A balanced mind like Renan's could not be embarrassed with the portable pharmacies and oculist's prescriptions, complete with appropriate ointments with which German criticism is overloaded.[3] The phrase that replaces all this is famous, "Who would dare to say that in many cases, always excepting certain peculiar injuries, the touch of a gracious woman is not equal to all the resources of pharmacy? The mere pleasure of seeing her cures. She gives only a smile, a hope, but these are not in vain."[4] Which explains why your daughter is no longer dumb!

[1] p. 124.

[2] p. 151.

[3] It is rather surprising then to read in the concluding considerations on our Lord, "Our laws upon the illegal exercise of medicine would alone have sufficed to cut short his career," p. 242.

[4] p. 151. Thus the *Everyman* translation. Renan said "une personne exquise."

But are madmen sensitive to a smile? Why not—on condition that you exaggerate nothing and that you know the East. " In our times, in Syria, they regard as mad or possessed by a demon (these two ideas are expressed by the same word *medjnoun*) people who are only somewhat eccentric. A gentle word often suffices in such cases to drive away the demon."[1] True, and blows are even more effective, for any self-willed person is called *medjnoun*. But there are also to be seen in Syria, furious madmen chained up in the porches of convents or churches, equally refractory under blows or soft words. It is of these madmen and of the most fearsome cases that the Gospels speak.[2]

" A mere sorcerer would not have effected a moral revolution like that of Jesus."[3] But then neither would it have been enough to be an exquisite person. No effect without a cause. Renan knew this, and he had recourse to the famous explanation, discredited as it is, of imposture—but he always found the word itself too severe for his indulgent judgment.

In the preface to the thirteenth edition, and in the appendix on St. John's Gospel, he expresses himself as crudely as his convention of sparing words and people permitted. Here is his definition of the receipt for a miracle: " A miracle in other words supposes three conditions: (1) the credulity of everybody; (2) a little obligingness on the part of a few; (3) the silent agreement of the chief author."[4]

Here we see again what was at the bottom of Renan's mind. This theory made the others

[1] p. 153.
[2] Matthew viii, 28, etc.
[3] p. 154.
[4] p. xxvii, French edition.

unnecessary, but doubtless he did not want to tear out some pleasantly written pages which might, moreover, produce their effect. A clever barrister makes an individual appeal to each of the judges and jurymen. His philosophy, too, perceived a truth in the light struck out by contrasts and even by contradictions. One can only conclude with M. de Séailles that "by giving all possible explanations he ends by giving none."[1] Positively, a few small miracles are not *de trop* as a means of escape from one great miracle. "The greatest miracle had been [*êut été*] his refusal to perform any."[2] Is this serious?

Renan's *Life of Jesus* marks a date in the history of religious ideas in France. It was scripture criticism for the first time reaching the general public. And this criticism came from Germany. It was almost exactly a century since Reimarus had violently scandalised his contemporaries by making Christianity the result of a fraud, not by a piece of elegant jesting as in France, but by calling upon his Oriental learning. Protestantism, more or less believing, had preferred to have recourse to the naturalist explanation of the supernatural. After the "myth" exegesis of Strauss, who reduced Jesus to nothing but a sort of phantom, German criticism had questioned the sources anew, recognised the solidly historical foundations and written the life of a wise and religious Christ.

[1] *Ernest Renan*, p. 137. [2] p. 155.

At this moment Renan came on the scene. He did not begin again with critical studies which in his judgment were already completed, but neither did he adhere to any one hypothesis. He claimed rather to replace them all by a bold but harmonious synthesis. German learning forms his foundation, but no more. The building is entirely his own work and he breathed into it the breath of enthusiasm by writing it on the hillsides of Galilee. If the conception is French how much more French is the form, so clean cut in its textual argument, so picturesque, so living and concrete in its pictures. So true is this that it may almost be said that Renan, by taking possession at one blow of all the learned German preparations, barred the road to the German invasion. This is made a reproach in the mouth of M. Schweitzer, but others honour Renan for it. Did things happen in the way put forward by this distinguished critic? It was all before the war, and we did not realise what was happening, but the Germans knew well enough that their seed was falling on French ground.

It was only a sowing as yet, says Schweitzer, spread by the theological school of Strasbourg, Reuss, Colani, Reville, Scherer, with the collaboration of Michel Nicolas de Montauban and Gustave d'Eichthal. Neffstzer, the editor of *Le Temps* backed them up in the literary world of Paris. The *Revue Germanique* was their ally. But Renan, they said, "in publishing too soon and in too superficial a fashion the ideas of the critical school, annihilated its unhurried labour."[1] Doubtless he did hamper the penetration into France of the German religious culture in all its crudity, but would it ever have acquired such an empire without the charm lent to it by the Breton magician?

The seduction of the book is undeniable: everyone agrees on the writer's gifts. His learning is definite and firm, without injuring the general ideas which seem to arise quite naturally from the facts. The historical framework is well drawn: Judea in its Messianic ferment, in face of the Roman stability, with occasional lights on other great religious movements such as Islam or Buddhism. The whole of history in fact is called before the reader to give its witness. The abuses of religious fanaticism, amazing instances of credulity, the perspective of a purer religion, all hold the reader in suspense. He inclines to the side on which he sees warm sympathy for beauty and virtue, and consideration even towards untruth, carried to the point of a scruple in naming it. The author profited by the wealth of a high culture and by his knowledge of the East which he freely bestowed on his readers.

The East of to-day seems with him to have come upon the scene for the first time in a *Life of Jesus.* Chateaubriand, so ardent for Athens and Sparta, was left cold by Jerusalem. Lamartine had almost forgotten the Bible. For Renan the spirit of the ancient histories brought the scenery to life; the earth trembled beneath the feet of Jesus, the lilies of Galilee bowed before him, the very sky opened

[1] *Geschichte der Leben-Jesu-Forschung,* p. 190.

as in the days of Jacob, and the stars twinkled joyfully on his slumbers. All was enchantment.

For the first time, too, a subject of edification was approached by a critical historian.

The critic loudly announced his uncertainties and hesitations as a historian, but all the more easily imposed on the world the conclusions of so prolonged a study, so conscientious, so anxious not to assert too much, when he tranquilly stated, "Jesus was born at Nazareth . . . his father Joseph."

To anyone *au courant* of the German learning his critical conclusions were moderate. He seemed to feel responsible for an incomparable literary treasure deposited in his hands. In love with the naïve beauty of the two first gospels he was not insensible to the more studied attraction of the third. Even of the fourth gospel treated so harshly by Strauss he desired to abandon nothing except the tiresome discourses—and even in these he knew how to find pearls. How much he hated to think the writers were in bad faith!

This immense sympathy was most of all evoked by the personality of his hero. But little more and he would have asked pardon for his favouritism, so strongly he felt that he had decided to raise him as high as poor human nature permitted. How could a critic be accused of hostility who, carried away by admiration, went so far as to find excuses for dishonest actions? Truly if he no longer believed he had done everything he could to believe and to remain faithful to his old ideal.

But he showed too much zeal over this. Shall we dare to speak of insincerity?[1] It would be imitating the man himself to make the reproach penetrate farther by veiling it. In the domain of pure history it is probably truer to accuse him of hesitation, and the oscillations of a mind which had undertaken to reconcile the irreconcilable. He could not at the same time, destroy the credit of the synoptic gospels, and make use of them in constructing solid history, write such history when he was inclined to sacrifice facts to an æsthetic impression, weave in one pattern learning and fantasy, praise and depreciation. While the Germans were devoting all their energies to deciding on the historical development of Christ, Renan laughed at everybody by describing a whole period of his ministry unknown by the historical sources, while he drew its features freely from those sources. And it was not enough to divide these years into two parts, one gay with the début of the "charmer," the other graver from his transformation into a "sombre giant." Besides this he allowed himself to generalise over the episodes in order to heighten the colouring of his pastoral. Jesus was only a man, yet at certain moments he was truly the Son of God. He had always known himself to be the Messiah of the Kingdom—yet it was only an error passing through his mind. There is a constant clash of contradictions,

[1] Schweitzer does not hesitate: "Great insincerity is shown from the beginning to the end of the book," op. laud., p. 192, and he quotes the judgment of Luthardt, "He lacks a moral conscience." One would not quote Germans against anyone else, but Renan *did* admire them so much!

and one hesitates to make use of them, so evident is it that the author has willed them and finds amusement in these little games.

He is amusing himself—yet he does not smile, or smiles only with pursed lips. For he knows quite well how serious the subject is, and that his tribunal of readers are not inclined to laugh. He knows he is leading those readers to a condemnatory verdict. It may be that Renan was in good faith in his denial of Christ's divinity. Of that God alone is the judge. But he has his responsibility as a writer. It is impossible to read him attentively without feeling that he is not sincere in his admiration for the Christ whose character he has studied so minutely. He admired Him, he loved Him in the seminary. He believed that he still loved Him when he left the Church. If, when writing His life, he still felt at moments the passing impression of the old affection he had by then made up his mind to sacrifice even Christ's honour as a man. He excuses Him—and the excuses are not honest; they have no bearing on the accusations, or they leave them unanswered. Renan is betraying his client. It may be said that that is all that can be done by the defender of a lost cause. But who took more trouble to lose it? In doing disservice to Our Lord he was winning in public opinion the cause of his own infidelity.

And what is the meaning of that emotional farewell on the tomb of Jesus which he believes he has sealed for ever: "Rest now in Thy glory, noble pioneer! Thy work is done; Thy divinity founded."[1]

[1] p. 227.

Very pretty! But if this is a pleasantry, it may be said, it is not a lie; the irony only conceals the meaning for those who cannot read. So be it, but the populace does not understand irony. Why was the *Vie Populaire* written, for the advantage of pious souls? Strange book of a subtle and perverse charm bringing a shudder to upright hearts!

How came it that Frenchmen, definite in mind, upright in heart, have been so sensible of this charm? We must admit that it is a disquieting symptom. And the saddest thing is that Renan's popularity began when, having laughed at everybody, he began to laugh at himself. It was forgotten that he was a "spoilt priest" until he cried it on the house tops—and then men found amusement in hearing him say it.

A superficial and light-minded society, too light to be firm even in its denials, enjoyed with all the passion it could put into the act, with the enthusiasm of a caprice, a negation which in a pleasant manner cast doubts on itself. Such readers knew Renan only as a dilettante inviting them to pleasure, and they had their laugh in reading him without asking if he was laughing at them. They did not understand the real passion, dominating and constant, which animated him in his denial of Christianity, a passion which does not merely accord with this scepticism, but which is rather the secret of it.

Commonly the historian clings to solutions which have cost him nights of toil. Renan worked hard yet he seems to cling to nothing. And in fact he does cling to nothing in questions about events and their sequence, characters and their probability—all, in one word, that goes to make up history. All solutions are equally good, and there can never be enough, provided they lead the reader to conclude that the supernatural has no existence and that therefore Renan was not mistaken.

For a long time yet France will see equally determined efforts to drag Jesus Christ down from her altars. Restored to her own free genius she will no longer, we hope, take pleasure in ironic and disloyal negation veiled under a show of respect.

www.ingramcontent.com/pod-product-compliance
Lightning Source LLC
LaVergne TN
LVHW020638100826
845148LV00012B/2224

* 9 7 8 1 6 0 6 0 8 3 9 2 5 *